Electrical Installation Calculations

VOLUME 3

by

A. J. WATKINS
B.Sc., B.Sc.(Aston), C.Eng., M.I.E.E.

SECOND EDITION

prepared by

RUSSELL K. PARTON

*Formerly Head of Department of Electrical
and Motor Vehicle Engineering, The Reid Kerr College, Paisley*

Edward Arnold
A member of the Hodder Headline Group
LONDON   MELBOURNE   AUCKLAND

First published in Great Britain 1970
Reprinted 1971, 1973, 1979, 1981, 1982, 1984, 1986, 1990, 1991
Second edition 1993
Reprinted 1994

British Library Cataloguing in Publication Data

Watkins, A. J.
 Electrical installation Calculations. –
 Vol. 3. – 2Rev.ed
 I. Title II. Parton, Russell K.
 621.30151

ISBN 0-340-57260-4

Typeset in Times by Anneset Phototypesetters.
Printed and bound in Great Britain for Edward Arnold, a division
of Hodder Headline Plc, 338 Euston Road, London NW1 3BH
by Athenæum Press Ltd, Newcastle upon Tyne.

PREFACE
TO THE SECOND EDITION

This book, together with Volumes 1 and 2, completes the series of books intended for students of electrical work. It is essentially a book of examples to co-ordinate the technology and calculations of the City and Guilds of the London Institute syllabuses in Electrical Installation Work (scheme 236). Volumes 1 and 2 satisfied the needs of Parts 1 and 2 and Volume 3 is aimed at Part 3 (Course C). The book is also suitable for students following BTEC and SCOTVEC electrical installation schemes, aimed at an NVQ in electrical installation. Representative examples are worked and a selection of problems, with answers, is provided to help the student to practice the techniques involved.

In this the second edition, the content has been revised to take into account syllabus revisions and changed or up-dated terminology. It also utilises the 16th edition of the IEE Wiring Regulations and certain of the IEE supporting material to the 16th edition. In common with Volumes 1 and 2 the revision has also taken into account British Standards (BS 5775) and International Electrotechnical Commission (IEC) publication 27, thus the 'preferred' symbol U replaces the traditional symbol V which has been widely used for potential difference. The symbol V now being the preferred symbol for unit of potential. Thus U_s (quantity of supply voltage) = 240 V (i.e. 240 units of voltage).

Certain material from the other two volumes has been included where it was felt to be essential to enable readers to further study the subject.

The publishers are grateful to the City and Guilds of London Institute for permission to use various questions from past examinations. The CGLI accepts no responsibility for the answers quoted for these questions.

Gratitude is also expressed to the Institution of Electrical Engineers for permission to make use of data from the 16th edition of the Wiring Regulations (Regulations for Electrical Installations) and from certain other IEE publications.

Kilmacolm
1992   R.K.P.

CONTENTS

DIRECT CURRENT CIRCUIT CALCULATIONS

References: **Ohm's law.**   **Simultaneous equations.**
           Kirchhoff's laws.

Working Statement of Kirchhoff's Laws.

1. The total current flowing towards any point in a circuit is equal to the total current flowing away from it.
   e.g.

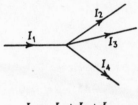

$$I_1 = I_2 + I_3 + I_4$$

2. The sum of the voltage drops taken round a circuit is equal to the e.m.f. acting in the circuit.
   e.g.

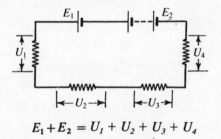

$$E_1 + E_2 = U_1 + U_2 + U_3 + U_4$$

Examples

A. Find the current in each resistor.

Label the currents as shown on the diagram.

1

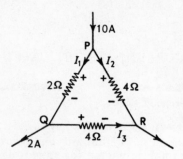

Applying Law 1 at P,

$$I_1 + I_2 = 10 \qquad (i)$$

at Q $\qquad I_3 + 2 = I_1$

or $\qquad I_1 - I_3 = 2 \qquad (ii)$

Applying Law 2 to the closed loop PRQ

$$4I_2 - 4I_3 - 2I_1 = 0 \qquad (iii)$$

Note carefully the minus signs which allow for the fact that the voltage drops across I_1 and I_3 have polarities opposite to that across I_2.

From equation (i)

$$I_2 = 10 - I_1 \qquad (iv)$$

from equation (ii)

$$I_3 = I_1 - 2 \qquad (v)$$

substituting for I_2 and I_3 in equation (iii)

$$4(10 - I_1) - 4(I_1 - 2) - 2I_1 = 0$$

$$40 - 4I_1 - 4I_1 + 8 - 2I_1 = 0$$

$$48 - 10I_1 = 0$$

or $\qquad 48 = 10I_1$

$$\therefore \ I_1 = \frac{48}{10}$$

$$= \underline{4 \cdot 8 \text{A}}$$

2

substituting in equation (iv) $I_2 = 10 - 4 \cdot 8$

$$= \underline{5 \cdot 2A}$$

substituting in equation (v) $I_3 = 4 \cdot 8 - 2$

$$= \underline{2 \cdot 8A}$$

Check at R where $I_2 + I_3 = 8$

$$5 \cdot 2 + 2 \cdot 8 = 8$$

Currents determined for each part of the circuit have the values shown above and directions as indicated on the circuit diagram.

B. Write down a set of simultaneous equations for the network shown.

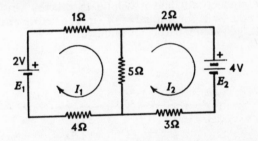

Imagine independent currents I_1 and I_2 to circulate in a *clockwise* direction as shown. The part of the circuit carrying the current I_1 is called Mesh 1, that part carrying the current I_2 is called Mesh 2. An e.m.f. is said to be positive if it acts in the same direction as the assumed current. For example E_1 is positive, E_2 is negative.

Applying the second Kirchhoff law and remembering that

$$U = I \times R$$

Mesh 1 $\qquad E_1 = 1I_1 + 5I_1 + 4I_1 - 5I_2$

The last term allows for the voltage drop produced in the 5Ω resistor by the current I_2 which passes through

3

the resistor in the opposite direction to that of I_1. This equation simplifies to

$$2 = 10I_1 - 5I_2$$

Similarly for Mesh 2

$$-E_2 = 2I_2 + 3I_2 + 5I_2 - 5I_1$$

or

$$-4 = -5I_1 + 10I_2$$

Notice that the current terms have been rearranged so that they appear in number order from left to right. The two equations are now written together and labelled

$$2 = 10I_1 - 5I_2 \tag{1}$$
$$-4 = -5I_1 + 10I_2 \tag{2}$$

Before proceeding to solve the equations, a few examples of more complicated circuits will be illustrated. The student will find it helpful to practise writing out the equations for a number of circuits before attempting to solve for any particular example.

C.

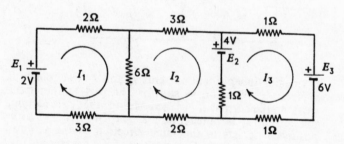

$E_1 = 2V$ positive sign

$E_2 = 4V$ negative sign for I_2 positive sign for I_3

$E_3 = 6V$ negative sign.

Mesh 1: $\quad 2 = 2I_1 + 6I_1 + 3I_1 - 6I_2$

or $\qquad\quad 2 = 11I_1 - 6I_2$

4

Mesh 2: $\quad -4 = 3I_2 + 1I_2 + 2I_2 + 6I_2 - 1I_3 - 6I_1$

or $\qquad -4 = -6I_1 + 12I_2 - 1I_3$

Mesh 3: $\quad 4 - 6 = 1I_3 + 1I_3 + 1I_3 - 1I_2$

or $\qquad -2 = -1I_2 + 3I_3$

and writing the three equations together

$$2 = 11I_1 - 6I_2 \qquad (1)$$

$$-4 = -6I_1 + 12I_2 - 1I_3 \qquad (2)$$

$$-2 = -1I_2 + 3I_3 \qquad (3)$$

D.

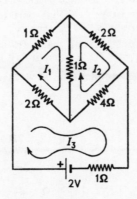

This is a Wheatstone Bridge.

$$E_1 = 0$$

$$E_2 = 0$$

$$E_3 = 2V \text{ positive sign.}$$

Mesh 1: $\quad 0 = 1I_1 + 1I_1 + 2I_2 - 1I_2 - 2I_3$

or $\qquad 0 = 4I_1 - 1I_2 - 2I_3$

Mesh 2: $\quad 0 = 2I_2 + 4I_2 + 1I_2 - 1I_1 - 4I_3$

or $\qquad 0 = -1I_1 + 7I_2 - 4I_3$

5

Mesh 3: $2 = 2I_3 + 4I_3 + 1I_3 - 2I_1 - 4I_2$

or $\qquad 2 = -2I_1 - 4I_2 + 7I_3$

and writing the equations together

$$0 = 4I_1 - 1I_2 - 2I_3 \qquad (1)$$

$$0 = -1I_1 + 7I_2 - 4I_3 \qquad (2)$$

$$2 = -2I_1 - 4I_2 + 7I_3 \qquad (3)$$

It is useful to note (i) that in this form, all the terms on the right-hand side are negative except for a diagonal row of positive terms; (ii) the equations may be remembered in words, for example in the case of Mesh 1:

e.m.f. = [(total resistance of mesh 1) × current I_1]
       − [(resistance of that part of mesh 1 carrying current I_2) × current I_2]
       − [(resistance of that part of mesh 1 carrying current I_3) × current I_3].

The following examples will be worked out fully.

E.

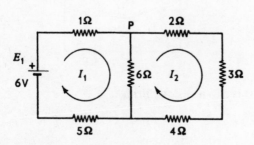

Calculate the p.d. across the 6-ohm resistor

$$E_1 = 6V \text{ positive sign}$$

$$E_2 = 0$$

Mesh 1: $6 = 1I_1 + 6I_1 + 5I_1 - 6I_2$

Mesh 2: $0 = 2I_2 + 3I_2 + 4I_2 + 6I_2 - 6I_1$

6

which are simplified and rewritten as

$$6 = 12I_1 - 6I_2 \qquad (1)$$
$$0 = -6I_1 + 15I_2 \qquad (2)$$

from equation (2)

$$6I_1 = 15I_2$$

or
$$I_1 = \frac{15I_2}{6} \qquad (3)$$

substituting in equation (1)

$$6 = 12 \times \frac{15I_2}{6} - 6I_2$$

or
$$6 = 30I_2 - 6I_2$$

or
$$6 = 24I_2$$

$$\therefore I_2 = \frac{6}{24} = \underline{0 \cdot 25A}$$

substituting in equation (3)

$$I_1 = \frac{15}{6} \cdot \frac{6}{24} = \underline{0 \cdot 625A}$$

The fact that both currents have positive signs means that the actual current flows in the same direction as the assumed current. The current in the 6-ohm resistor is

$$I_1 - I_2 = 0 \cdot 625 - 0 \cdot 25$$
$$= 0 \cdot 375A$$

Take care to insert the correct signs for I_1 and I_2.

The polarity of the battery ensures that this current flows from P to Q. The p.d. across the 6-ohm resistor is

$$U_6 = 0 \cdot 375 \times 6$$
$$= \underline{2 \cdot 25V}$$

P being at the higher potential (or P is positive with respect to Q).

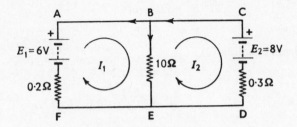

Find the current through each part of the circuit

E_1 is positive with respect to I_1

E_2 is negative with respect to I_2

Mesh 1: $\qquad 6 = 10 \cdot 2 I_1 - 10 I_2 \qquad\qquad$ (1)

Mesh 2: $\qquad -8 = -10 I_1 + 10 \cdot 3 I_2 \qquad$ (2)

from (1) $\qquad I_2 = \dfrac{10 \cdot 2 I_1 - 6}{10}$

$\qquad\qquad\qquad = 1 \cdot 02 I_1 - 0 \cdot 6 \qquad\qquad\quad$ (3)

substitute in (2) $-8 = -10 I_1 + 10 \cdot 3 (1 \cdot 02 I_1 - 0 \cdot 6)$

$\qquad\qquad\qquad -8 = -10 I_1 + 10 \cdot 5 I_1 - 6 \cdot 18$

$\qquad\qquad\qquad -8 = 0 \cdot 5 I_1 - 6 \cdot 18$

$\qquad\qquad\qquad I_1 = \dfrac{6 \cdot 18 - 8}{0 \cdot 5}$

$\qquad\qquad\qquad I_1 = \underline{-3 \cdot 64 \text{A}}$

This is the actual current in the parts of the circuit BA, AF and FE. The minus sign indicates that the actual current flows in the reverse direction to the assumed current I_1. We shall indicate the actual current as $I_{BA} = I_{AF} = I_{FE} = 3 \cdot 64$A, the order of the letters then indicates the direction of the actual current. Substitute for I_1 in (3)

$\qquad\qquad I_2 = 1 \cdot 02 (-3 \cdot 64) - 0 \cdot 6$

$\qquad\qquad\quad = -3 \cdot 71 - 0 \cdot 6$

$\qquad\qquad I_2 = \underline{-4 \cdot 31 \text{A}}$

8

The minus sign again shows that the actual current flow is opposite to that of I_2, that is

$$I_{ED} = I_{DC} = I_{CB} = 4\cdot31A$$

As an alternative to the method of example E, mark on the diagram say at B the actual directions of current flow using small arrows as shown. The current in the 10-ohm resistor is then found by applying Kirchhoff's first law at point B;

thus current in 10-ohm resistor

$$= I_{BE} = I_{CB} - I_{BA}$$

or

$$= 4\cdot31 - 3\cdot64$$

$$= 0\cdot67A \text{ in direction from B to E.}$$

[The current must flow in this direction because both batteries have their positive terminals at the top.]

G. Two batteries connected in parallel are to be charged by connecting them in series with a $0\cdot8$-Ω resistor to a 20-V d.c. supply. Battery 1 has e.m.f. 12V and internal resistance $0\cdot2\Omega$. Battery 2 has e.m.f. 12V and internal resistance $0\cdot4\Omega$. Calculate the current taken from the supply and the current through each battery.

Circuit arrangement

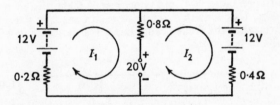

Mesh 1: $12 - 20 = 1I_1 - 0\cdot8I_2$

Mesh 2: $20 - 12 = -0\cdot8I_1 + 1\cdot2I_2$

or

$$-8 = I_1 - 0\cdot8I_2 \qquad (1)$$

$$8 = -0\cdot8I_1 + 1\cdot2I_2 \qquad (2)$$

from (1) $I_1 = 0.8I_2 - 8$ (3)

substituting for I_1 in (2)

$$8 = -0.8(0.8I_2 - 8) + 1.2I_2$$
$$8 = -0.64I_2 + 6.4 + 1.2I_2$$
$$8 - 6.4 = 0.56I_2$$
$$I_2 = \frac{1.6}{0.56}$$
$$= 2.85A$$

Thus battery 2 is being charged at the rate of 2·85A. Substituting for I_2 in (3)

$$I_1 = 0.8 \times \frac{1.6}{0.56} - 8$$
$$= -5.714A$$

Thus battery 1 is being charged at the rate of 5·714A. The supply current is thus

$$5.714 + 2.85 = \underline{8.564A}$$

H. A substation S feeds a d.c. distributor at 235V. Consumer X at 200m distance takes 120A, consumer Y at 450m distance takes 80A and consumer Z 600m distance takes 100A. Calculate the voltage at each consumer's terminals given that the feeder cable has a resistance of 0·08Ω per 1000m per core.

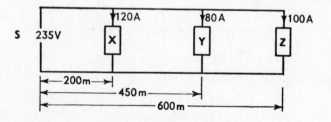

Applying the first Kirchhoff law:

Current in section YZ = 100A

Current in section XY = 100+80 = 180A

Current in section SX = 180+120 = 300A

Resistance of 1m of *double* core $= \dfrac{0.08}{1000} \times 2\Omega$

Resistance of section SX $= 200 \times \dfrac{0.08}{1000} \times 2$

$= 0.032\Omega$

Voltage drop in SX $= 300 \times 0.032$

$= 9.6V$

∴ voltage at X terminals $= 235 - 9.6$

$= 225.4V$

Resistance of section XY $= 250 \times \dfrac{0.08}{1000} \times 2$

$= 0.04\Omega$

volts drop in section XY $= 180 \times 0.04$

$= 7.2V$

voltage at Y terminals $= 225.4 - 7.2$

$= 218.2V$

Resistance of section YZ $= 150 \times \dfrac{0.08}{1000} \times 2$

$= 0.024\Omega$

volts drop in section YZ $= 100 \times 0.024$

$= 2.4V$

voltage at Z terminals $= 218.2 - 2.4$

$= 215.8V$

Correct to three significant figures the required voltages are thus—at X 225V

at Y 218V

at Z 216V

J. If the distributor of Example G be reconnected so as to form a ring circuit, calculate the current in each section and the voltage at each consumer's terminals.

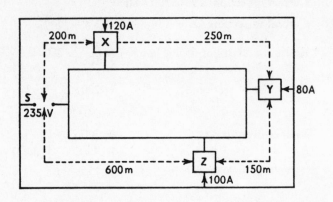

Applying the first Kirchhoff law and calling the current in section SX xA

then the current in section XY $= (x-120)$A

and current in section YZ $= (x-120-80)$
$= (x-200)$A

and current in section ZS $= (x-200-100)$
$= (x-300)$A

as before, resistance of SX $= 0.032\Omega$
∴ volts drop in section SX $= 0.032x$V

resistance of XY $= 0.04\Omega$
∴ volts drop in section XY $= 0.04(x-120)$V

resistance of YZ $= 0.024\Omega$
∴ volts drop in section YZ $= 0.024(x-200)$V

resistance of section ZS $= 600 \times \dfrac{0.08 \times 2}{1000}$
$= 0.096\Omega$

volts drop in section ZS $= 0.096(x-300)$V

12

There is no resultant e.m.f. round the ring circuit formed by either conductor since both start and finish at S. Thus

$$0·032x + 0·04(x - 120) + 0·024(x - 200) + 0·096(x - 300) = 0$$
$$0·032x + 0·04x - 4·8 + 0·024x - 4·8 + 0·096x - 28·8 = 0$$

$$0·192x = 38·4$$

$$x = \frac{38·4}{0·192}$$

$$= 200A$$

i.e. the current in section SX = 200A

Volts drop in section SX	$= 200 \times 0·032$
	$= 6·4V$
so that the voltage at X	$= 235 - 6·4$
	$= 228·6V$
Current in section XY	$= x - 120$
	$= 200 - 120 = 80A$
volts drop in section XY	$= 80 \times 0·04$
	$= 3·2V$
so that the voltage at Y	$= 228·6 - 3·2$
	$= 225·4V$
Current in section YZ	$= x - 200A$
	$= 200 - 200$
	$= 0$
The volts drop in YZ	$= 0$
and voltage at Z	$= 225·4V$
current in ZS	$= (x - 300)$
	$= 200 - 300$
	$= -100A$ (flowing in opposite direction)
volts drop in section ZS	$= -100 \times 0·096$
	$= -9·6V$ (a rise in voltage)
and the voltage at S	$= 225·4 - (-9·6)$
	$= 235·0$

To summarise, and correcting to three significant figures.

Current in SX = 200A, p.d. at X = 229V
Current in XY = 80A, p.d. at Y = 225V
Current in YZ = 0,   p.d. at Z = 225V
Current in ZS = 100A

Exercises 1

1. Write down sets of simultaneous equations for the following circuits. (Resistance values are all in ohms.)

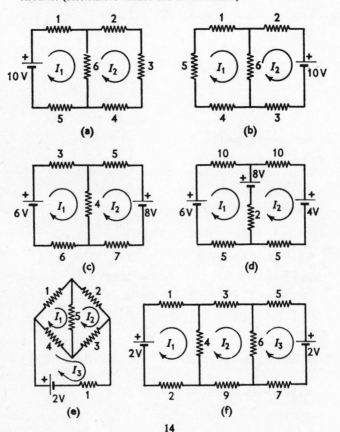

(a)

(b)

(c)

(d)

(e)

(f)

14

2. Find the current in each part of each circuit shown. (Resistance values are all in ohms.)

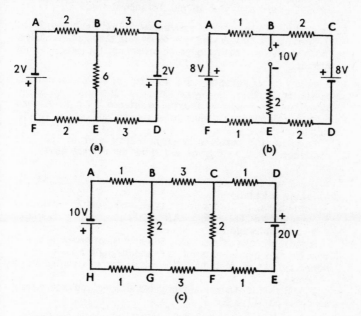

(a)

(b)

(c)

3. Find the current in section BD of the bridge circuit.

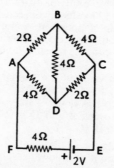

4. Two batteries are connected in parallel and together they supply current to a 10-Ω resistor connected across their terminals.

One battery has e.m.f. 6V and internal resistance 1Ω, the other has e.m.f. 6V and internal resistance 2Ω. Calculate the current through the resistor and the p.d. between its ends.

5. The circuit of example 4 is rearranged so that the batteries are charged from a 10-volt supply in series with the 10-ohm resistor. Calculate the current through each battery and the total charging current.

6. A battery of cells of total e.m.f. 40 volts and with total internal resistance 2 ohms, is connected in parallel with a second battery of 44 volts and internal resistance 4 ohms. A load resistance of 6 ohms is connected across the ends of the parallel circuit.

Calculate the currents in each battery and in the load resistance. Draw a diagram and show the current directions.
(C & G)

7. Write down Kirchhoff's laws, and use them in working the following calculation.

Four resistances are connected in a closed circuit in the form of a square ABCD, where AB = 20 ohms, BC = 30 ohms, CD = 40 ohms and DA = 50 ohms.

A galvanometer of resistance 80 ohms is connected across B and D, and a cell of e.m.f. 2V and negligible resistance is connected across A and C. The whole forms an unbalanced Wheatstone Bridge.

Find the value of current in the galvanometer, and show clearly its direction. (C & G)

8. Four resistances AB, BC, AD and DC, are connected together to form a closed square ABCD. The known resistance values are: AD—12 ohms, AB—35 ohms, and DC—12 ohms.

A d.c. supply of 120 volts is connected to A and C so that current enters the combination at A and leaves at C. A high-resistance voltmeter is connected between B and C, and whilst carrying negligible current, registers a voltage drop of 10 volts from B to C.

(a) Calculate the value of the resistance BC, and the total current taken from the supply.

(b) Calculate also the value of BC, such that the potential difference between B and D is in the reverse direction, i.e. from D to B. (C & G)

9. A d.c. 2-wire distributor AD is supplied at end A at 230V and loads are taken from it as follows:

at B 50m from A 60A
at C 200m from A 80A
at D 300m from A 100A

The resistance of each core is 0.2Ω per 1000m. Calculate the current in each section of cable and the voltage at B, C and D.

10. The distributor of question 9 is converted to a ring circuit by joining D to A with a 300-m length of the same cable. Calculate the current in each section and the voltage at B, C and D.

11. Write down Kirchhoff's laws and use them in working the following calculation:

A 2-wire ring main is 600m long, and is supplied at a point P with direct current at 240V. A load of 70A is taken from the main at point Q, 150m from P in one direction, and a further load of 50A is taken at a point R, 300m from P in the other direction. The resistance of the main is $0.4\Omega/1000$m of single core.

Find the currents in value and direction in each section of the ring main, and calculate the voltages at points Q and R.

(C & G)

12. A 3-wire d.c. system supplies power to two adjacent workshops by means of a 3-core aluminium cable. The voltage at the main switchboard is maintained at 240/0/240V.

Workshop A takes 200A from positive and neutral, and workshop B takes 250A from neutral and negative. The resistance of each outer core of the cable is 0.238Ω and that of the inner core is 0.396Ω.

Show on a suitable diagram the values and directions of the currents in the cable, and calculate the voltages at A and B respectively.

Describe in general terms what would happen if the neutral core became disconnected.

ALTERNATING CURRENT CIRCUIT CALCULATIONS I

SERIES CIRCUIT

References: **Inductive reactance.**   **Phasor diagrams.**
Capacitive reactance.   **Quadratic equations.**
Impedance.
Power and power factor.
Resonance.

Consider a circuit consisting of resistance inductance and capacitance in series:

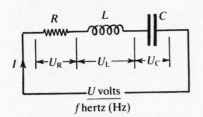

R is resistance (ohm)
L is inductance (henry)
C is capacitance (microfarad)

The current is the same at all places in the circuit.
The voltage drop across the resistance is $U_R = I \times R$ in phase with the current.
The voltage drop across the inductance is $U_L = I \times X_L$ where $X_L = 2\pi f L$. This voltage drop leads on the current by 90°.
The voltage drop across the capacitor is $U_C = I \times X_C$ where

$$X_C = \frac{10^6}{2\pi f C}$$

This voltage drop lags on the current by 90°.
The supply voltage is *U*.
The phasor diagram is usually shown thus:

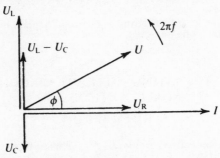

Figure A

The current is drawn first as the reference phasor. The resultant of U_L and U_C since they are in antiphase is found by subtracting the smaller from the larger. The supply voltage *U* is drawn by combining U_R and $U_L - U_C$ (or $U_C - U_L$ in the manner described in volume 2.

18

ϕ is the phase angle between current and supply voltage. $\cos \phi$ is the overall power factor of the circuit. Figure A shows the phasor diagram for an overall lagging power factor. This occurs when U_L is greater than U_C.

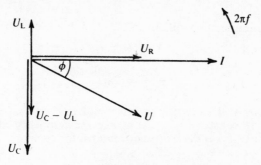

Figure B

Figure B shows the case of an overall leading power factor which occurs when U_C is greater than U_L.

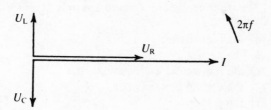

Figure C

Figure C shows the case when $U_L = U_C$, here $U = U_R$.

The phase angle between current and supply voltage is zero giving a power factor of 1 or unity ($\because \cos 0 = 1$). This is the series resonant condition, the current in the circuit has its maximum value, being limited only by the resistance.

The impedance of the general series circuit is given by

$$Z^2 = R^2 + (X_L - X_C)^2$$

or
$$Z^2 = R^2 + (X_C - X_L)^2$$

(simply taking the smaller from the larger)
and from either formula it is seen that when $X_C = X_L$

$$Z = R$$

For the resonant condition

$$X_C = X_L$$

$$\frac{10^6}{2\pi fC} = 2\pi fL$$

and this is achieved either by adjusting L or C or both with the frequency constant or by adjusting the frequency alone in which case if f_r is the frequency required for resonance

$$f_r = \frac{10^3}{2\pi\sqrt{(LC)}} \text{ Hz}$$

Examples

A. A 10-Ω resistor, a 100-μF capacitor and an inductor of 0·15 H are connected in series to a supply at 240 V 50 Hz. Calculate:

    (*a*) the impedance;

    (*b*) the current;

    (*c*) the p.d. across each component;

    (*d*) the overall power factor;

    (*e*) the power.

Draw the phasor diagram.

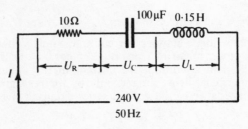

$$X_L = 2\pi f L$$
$$= 2\pi \times 50 \times 0.15$$
$$X_C = \frac{10^6}{2\pi f C}$$
$$= 47.2\Omega$$
$$= \frac{10^6}{2\pi \times 50 \times 100}$$
$$= 31.8\Omega$$

$$Z^2 = R^2 + (X_L - X_C)^2$$
$$= 10^2 + (47.2 - 31.8)^2$$
$$= 10^2 + (15.4)^2$$
$$= 100 + 237.2$$
$$Z = \sqrt{337.2}$$
$$= \underline{18.37\Omega} \qquad (a)$$

$$I = \frac{U}{Z}$$
$$= \frac{240}{18.37}$$
$$= \underline{13.06\text{A}} \qquad (b)$$

$$U_R = I \times R$$
$$= 13.06 \times 10$$
$$= \underline{130.6\text{V}}$$

$$U_C = I \times X_C$$
$$= 13.06 \times 31.8$$
$$= \underline{415\text{V}}$$

$$U_L = I \times X_L$$
$$= 13.06 \times 47.2$$
$$= \underline{616\text{V}} \qquad (c)$$

21

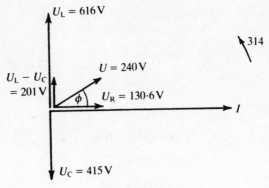

Phasor Diagram

From the phasor diagram

$$\tan \phi = \frac{U_L - U_C}{U_R}$$

$$= \frac{616 - 415}{130 \cdot 6}$$

$$= \frac{201}{130 \cdot 6}$$

$$= 1 \cdot 539$$

$$\phi = 56° \ 59'$$

power factor $= \cos \phi$ (lag)

$$= 0 \cdot 545 \qquad (d)$$

Total power

$$P = UI \cos \phi$$

$$= 240 \times 13 \cdot 06 \times 0 \cdot 545$$

$$= 1708 \text{W} \qquad (e)$$

B. Calculate tne value to which the frequency of the previous circuit would have to be adjusted in order for the power factor to be unity and determine the current at this frequency.

Unity power factor is achieved at the resonant condition, the required frequency is

$$f_r = \frac{10^3}{2\pi\sqrt{(LC)}}$$

$$= \frac{10^3}{2\pi\sqrt{(0\cdot15 \times 100)}}$$

$$= \frac{10^3}{2\pi \times \sqrt{15}}$$

$$= \frac{10^3}{2\pi \times 3\cdot873}$$

$$= \underline{41\cdot1 \text{ Hz}}$$

At this frequency the two values of reactance are equal and the current is limited only by the resistance. The current is then

$$I_r = \frac{U}{R}$$

$$= \frac{240}{10}$$

$$= \underline{24A}$$

C. A coil has resistance 80Ω and inductance $0\cdot318$ H. Calculate the value of a capacitor which if connected in series with the coil to a 50-Hz sinusoidal supply will cause the same current to flow as if the coil alone were connected to the same supply. Draw the phasor diagrams and determine the overall power factor.

Reactance of coil

$$X_L = 2\pi f L$$

$$= 2\pi \times 50 \times 0\cdot318$$

$$= 100\Omega$$

Impedance of coil alone

$$Z^2 = R^2 + X_L^2$$

$$= 80^2 + 100^2$$

$$Z = 128\Omega$$

23

Impedance of the coil and capacitor in series

$$Z^2 = R^2 + (X_C - X_L)^2$$

and for the same current these two values must be the same, therefore

$$X_C - X_L = X_L$$

(Note that if we put $X_L - X_C = X_L$, $X_C = 0$ which does not satisfy our problem.)

and

$$X_C = 2X_L$$

$$\frac{10^6}{2\pi f C} = 2 \times 2\pi f L$$

$$\therefore C = \frac{10^6}{2 \times 2^2 \pi^2 \times 50^2 \times 0\cdot318}$$

$$= \underline{15\cdot9 \ \mu F}$$

Phasor Diagrams

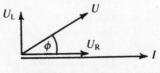

(a) for coil alone.

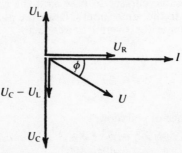

(b) for coil and capacitor in series.

The power factor has the same value for both circuit conditions, in the first case it is lagging, in the second case leading. Its value is obtained as follows:

$$\cos \phi = \frac{R}{Z} \quad \begin{array}{l} \text{(resistance of coil)} \\ \text{(impedance of coil)} \end{array}$$

$$= \frac{80}{128}$$

$$= \underline{0 \cdot 625}$$

D. A coil has resistance 80Ω and inductance $0 \cdot 318$ H. It is connected in series with a capacitor of $158 \, \mu$F to a sinusoidal supply of 256V at variable frequency. Calculate the two values of frequency for which the current in the circuit is 2A.

Impedance $\qquad Z = \dfrac{U}{I}$

$$= \frac{256}{2}$$

$$= 128\Omega$$

$$Z^2 = R^2 + (X_L - X_C)^2$$

$$(X_L - X_C)^2 = Z^2 - R^2$$

$$= 128^2 - 80^2$$

$$= 10\,000$$

$$X_L - X_C = 100 \qquad \text{(i)}$$

$$[\text{or } X_C - X_L = 100 \quad \text{(ii)}]$$

$$2\pi f L - \frac{10^6}{2\pi f C} = 100$$

$$2\pi \times 0 \cdot 318 f^2 - \frac{10^6}{2\pi \times 158} = 100f \quad \text{(after multiplying by} f)$$

$$2f^2 - 1000 = 100f$$

or $\quad 2f^2 - 100f - 1000 = 0$

This is a quadratic equation which is found in the general form

$$ax^2 + bx + c = 0$$

where a, b and c are constants and its two solutions are given by

$$x = \frac{-b \pm \sqrt{b^2 - 4ac}}{2a}$$

here $x = f$, $a = 2$, $b = -100$, $c = -1000$,

$$\therefore f = \frac{100 \pm \sqrt{(-100)^2 - (4 \times 2 \times -100)}}{2 \times 2}$$

$$= \frac{100 \pm \sqrt{10\,000 + 8000}}{4}$$

$$= \frac{100 \pm \sqrt{18\,000}}{4}$$

$$= 58 \cdot 6 \text{ and } -8 \cdot 6$$

The negative frequency is meaningless but $-8 \cdot 6$ satisfies the condition (ii) above.

The required frequencies are thus $58 \cdot 6$ and $8 \cdot 6$ Hz.

Exercises 2

1. A resistor of 15Ω, an inductor of $0 \cdot 0318$ H and a 150-μF capacitor are connected in series to a 240-V sinusoidal supply at 50 Hz. Calculate:
   - (a) the impedance of the whole circuit;
   - (b) the current;
   - (c) the power factor;
   - (d) the voltage across each component.

   Draw the phasor diagram to scale.

2. When a coil is connected to a 240-V d.c. supply a current of 2A flows. When it is connected to a 240-V a.c. supply at 50 Hz the current is 1A. Calculate the current which flows when the same coil is connected in series with a capacitor of 30 μF to the same a.c. supply.

3. The following table refers to a circuit consisting of an inductance $0 \cdot 318$ H, a resistor of 50Ω and a 20-μF capacitor all connected in series to a 200-V sinusoidal supply of variable frequency. Complete the table and plot curves showing the current in the circuit and the p.d. across each component plotted against frequency.

frequency Hz	20	30	40	50	60	70	80
$X_L = 2\pi fL$							
$X_c = 10^6/2\pi fC$							
Z							
I							
U_L							
U_R							
U_c							

4. Complete the table which refers to inductance and capacitance in series and the frequency of resonance.

Inductance (H)	0·3		1·5	1	
Capacitance (μF)	25	40		50	30
Resonant frequency (Hz)		50	100		250

5. A resistance of 24Ω, a capacitance of 160 μF and an inductance of 0·16 H are connected in series with each other. A supply at 240V, 50 Hz, is applied to the ends of the combination.

Calculate:

   (a) the current in the circuit;

   (b) the potential differences across each element of the circuit;

   (c) the frequency to which the supply would need to be changed so that the current would be at unity power-factor, and find the current at this frequency.

6. A coil of insulated wire of resistance 8Ω and inductance 0·03 H is connected to an a.c. supply at 240V, 50 Hz.

Calculate:

   (a) The current, the power, and the power factor;

   (b) The value (in microfarads) of a capacitor which, when connected in series with the above coil, causes no change in the values of current and power taken from the supply.

7. A coil has inductance 0·223 H and resistance 50Ω. Find the two values of capacitance which when connected in series with the coil to a 240-V 50-Hz supply will cause a current of 3A to flow and calculate the corresponding power factors.

8. A circuit consists of a resistor of 35 ohms, an inductor of negligible resistance and a capacitor connected in series. A current of 2 ampères flows in the circuit when it is connected to a 50-hertz sinusoidal supply. A voltmeter connected in turn across the inductor and capacitor reads 200 volts and 130 volts respectively. Calculate:

    (i) the value of the inductance;

    (ii) the value of the capacitance;

    (iii) the supply voltage.

Draw the phasor diagram to scale.   (C & G)

9. A coil of resistance 100 ohms and inductance 0·244 henry is connected in series with a capacitor of 30 microfarad to a 100-volt sinusoidal supply of variable frequency. Calculate the two values of frequency for which the current is 0·707 ampère.

10. An inductor of 0·5 henry is connected in series with a capacitor of 72 microfarad and a resistor of unknown value.

Calculate:

    (i) the resonant frequency of the circuit;

    (ii) the value of the resistor so that at resonance the current taken from a 100-volt supply shall be 4 ampères;

    (iii) the p.d. across each component at resonance.

ALTERNATING CURRENT CIRCUIT CALCULATIONS II

PARALLEL CIRCUIT

References: **Inductive reactance.**   **Capacitive reactance.**
Impedance.
Phasor resolution and combination.

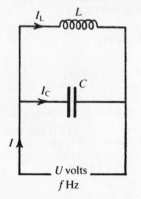

Consider a circuit consisting of inductance and capacitance in parallel.

L is a pure inductance (henry)

C is a pure capacitance (microfarad)

28

The same voltage is applied to each branch of the circuit. The current through the inductance is $I_L = U_{XL}$ where $X_L = 2\pi f L$. This current lags the voltage by 90°. The capacitor current is $I_C = U/X_C = 10^6/2\pi f C$. This current leads the voltage by 90°. The phasor diagram is usually drawn thus:

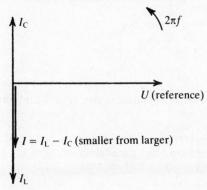

Usually the inductive branch possesses resistance:

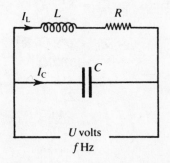

I_L lags the voltage U by some angle less than 90° depending upon the values of L and R (L and R form a series circuit).

29

The phasor diagram is

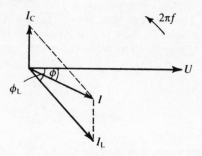

ϕ_L is the phase angle of the inductive branch and $\tan \phi_L = X_L/R$ (see volume 2).

The supply current is the phasor sum of I_C and I_L which is found by completing the parallelogram, ϕ is the phase angle between supply voltage and current.

Examples

A. A coil has resistance 25Ω and inductive reactance 20Ω. It is connected in parallel with a capacitor of reactance 40Ω to a 240-V a.c. supply. Determine the supply current and the overall power factor.

Coil impedance
$$Z_L^2 = R^2 + X_L^2$$
$$= 25^2 + 20^2$$
$$Z_L = \sqrt{25^2 + 20^2}$$
$$= 32 \cdot 02\Omega$$

Coil current
$$I_L = \frac{U}{Z_L}$$
$$= \frac{240}{32 \cdot 02}$$
$$= 7 \cdot 495A$$
$$= 7 \cdot 5A$$

Coil phase angle
is found from $\tan \phi_L = \dfrac{X_L}{R}$

30

$$= \frac{20}{25}$$
$$= 0 \cdot 8$$
$$\phi_L = 38° \ 39'$$

Capacitor Current $I_C = \dfrac{U}{X_C}$
$$= \frac{240}{40}$$
$$= 6A$$

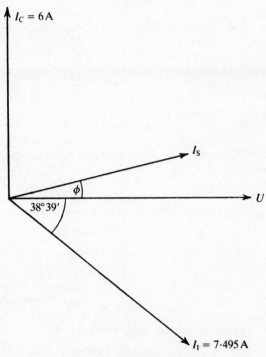

Phasor Diagram to Scale.

The supply current may be determined:

(a) graphically by constructing the phasor diagram to scale.

By measurement $I_S = 6A$ and $\cos \phi = 0.976$ leading or

(b) by calculation as follows:
The horizontal component of the coil current is

$$I_L \cos \phi_L = 7.5 \cos 38° 39'$$
$$= 7.5 \times 0.7810$$
$$= 5.858$$

The horizontal component of the capacitor current

$$= 0$$

The total horizontal component

$$X = 5.858 + 0$$
$$= 5.858$$

The vertical component of the capacitor current

$$= 6.0$$

The vertical component of the coil current is

$$-I_L \sin \phi_L = -7.5 \sin 38° 39'$$
$$= -7.5 \times 0.6246$$
$$= -4.685 \quad \text{(The minus sign because this component acts downwards.)}$$

• The total vertical component

$$Y = 6.0 - 4.685$$
$$= 1.315$$

The resultant current

$$I_S = \sqrt{X^2 + Y^2}$$
$$= \sqrt{5 \cdot 858^2 + 1 \cdot 315^2}$$
$$= \underline{6A}$$

The phase angle between the supply current and the voltage is given by

$$\tan \phi = \frac{Y}{X}$$

$$= \frac{1 \cdot 315}{5 \cdot 858}$$

$$= 0 \cdot 2247$$

$$\phi = 12° \, 40'$$

and the overall power factor is

$$\cos \phi = \cos 12° \, 40'$$
$$= \underline{0 \cdot 976 \text{ leading}}$$

B. A parallel circuit consists of two branches. Branch A has inductive reactance 100Ω and resistance $173 \cdot 2\Omega$ in series. Branch B has capacitive reactance $173 \cdot 2\Omega$ and resistance 100Ω in series. The supply to the circuit is 200V 50 Hz. Determine:

    (*a*) the supply current and the power factor;

    (*b*) the components of the equivalent series circuit.

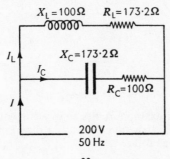

For the inductive branch

$$Z_L = \sqrt{R_L^2 + X_L^2}$$
$$= \sqrt{(173\cdot2)^2 + (100)^2}$$
$$= 200\Omega$$
$$I_L = \frac{U}{Z_L}$$
$$= \frac{200}{200} = 1\text{A}$$

The phase angle ϕ_L is found from

$$\tan \phi_L = \frac{X_L}{R} \quad \text{(see impedance triangle)}$$
$$= \frac{100}{173\cdot2}$$

and $\qquad \phi_L = 30° \quad \text{(lag)}$

For the capacitive branch

$$Z_C = \sqrt{R_C^2 + X_C^2}$$
$$= \sqrt{(100)^2 + (173\cdot2)^2}$$
$$= 200\Omega$$
$$I_C = \frac{U}{Z_C}$$
$$= \frac{200}{200} = 1\text{A}$$
$$\tan \phi_C = \frac{X_C}{R}$$
$$= \frac{173\cdot2}{100}$$
$$\phi_C = 60° \quad \text{(lead)}$$

Again as in example A the supply current may be determined by constructing the phasor diagram to scale or by calculation as follows:

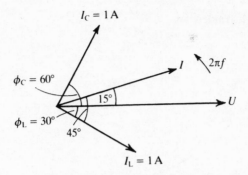

It will be observed that I_L and I_C are at right angles, their resultant can thus be found by applying Pythagoras Theorem directly:

$$I = \sqrt{I_C{}^2 + I_L{}^2}$$
$$= \sqrt{1^2 + 1^2}$$
$$= \sqrt{2} = \underline{1 \cdot 414A} \qquad (a)$$

Furthermore since $I_C = I_L$ their resultant lies at an angle of 45° to I_L. The phase angle between I and U is thus 45° − 30° = 15° (lead) and the power factor is

$$\cos \phi = \cos 15°$$
$$= \underline{0 \cdot 966 \text{ lead}} \qquad (a)$$

For the equivalent series circuit we require a circuit which takes a current of 1·414A at 0·966 power factor leading from a 200-V 50-Hz supply. The circuit will consist of a capacitor and resistor in series.

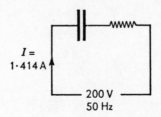

35

its impedance $Z = \dfrac{U}{I}$

$$= \frac{200}{1 \cdot 414}$$

$$= 141 \cdot 4\Omega$$

$\phi = 15°$, $\cos \phi = 0 \cdot 966$, $\sin \phi = 0 \cdot 2588$

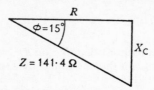

From the impedance triangle

$$\cos \phi = \frac{R}{Z}$$

$$0 \cdot 966 = \frac{R}{141 \cdot 4}$$

$$R = 141 \cdot 4 \times 0 \cdot 966$$

$$= \underline{136 \cdot 6\Omega}$$

$$\sin \phi = \frac{X_C}{Z}$$

$$0 \cdot 2588 = \frac{X_C}{141 \cdot 4}$$

$$X_C = 141 \cdot 4 \times 0 \cdot 2588$$

$$= 36 \cdot 59\Omega$$

$$X_C = \frac{10^6}{2\pi f C}$$

$$36 \cdot 59 = \frac{10^6}{2\pi \times 50 \times C}$$

$$C = \frac{10^6}{2\pi \times 50 \times 36 \cdot 59}$$

$$= \underline{87\ \mu F}$$

The equivalent circuit thus consists of a capacitor of $87 \cdot 4\ \mu F$ in series with a resistor of $136 \cdot 6\Omega$.   (b)

C. A coil has inductance $0 \cdot 318\,H$ and resistance 200Ω. A capacitor of value $3 \cdot 18\ \mu F$ is connected in parallel with the coil to a sinusoidal supply of variable frequency. Calculate the frequency at which the supply current and voltage are in phase.

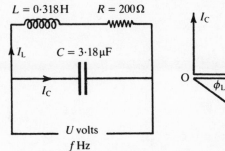
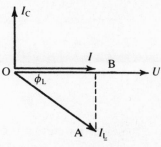

From the phasor diagram it is seen that for the supply current I to be in phase with the voltage U the vertical component of the coil current AB must be equal to the capacitor current.

Let f be the required frequency in Hz.

For the coil $X_L = 2\pi fL$
$$= 2\pi \times f \times 0 \cdot 318$$
$$= 2f$$

$$Z = \sqrt{R^2 + X_L{}^2}$$
$$= \sqrt{200^2 + (2f)^2}$$

and $$I_L = \frac{U}{\sqrt{(200^2 + (2f)^2)}}$$

37

From the triangle OAB $\dfrac{AB}{OA} = \sin \phi_L$

$$AB = OA \sin \phi_L$$
$$= I_L \sin \phi_L$$

ϕ_L is the phase angle of the coil circuit at the frequency f.

From the impedance triangle for the coil

$$\sin \phi_L = \frac{X_L}{Z_L}$$

$$\therefore \ AB = \frac{U}{\sqrt{(200^2 + (2f)^2)}} \times \frac{2f}{\sqrt{(200^2 + (2f)^2)}}$$
$$= \frac{2fU}{200^2 + (2f)^2}$$

The capacitor current is $I_C = \dfrac{U}{X_C}$

and $$X_C = \frac{10^6}{2\pi f C}$$

$$\therefore \ I_C = \frac{U}{10^6 / 2\pi f C}$$
$$= U \times \frac{2\pi f C}{10^6}$$
$$= U \times \frac{2\pi \times 3 \cdot 18 \times f}{10^6}$$
$$= \frac{2 \times U \times f}{10^5}$$

and $$\frac{2fU}{200^2 + (2f)^2} = \frac{2Uf}{10^5}$$

$$\therefore \quad 200^2 + 4f^2 = 10^5$$
$$4f^2 = 100\,000 - 40\,000$$
$$f^2 = \frac{60\,000}{4}$$
$$f = \sqrt{15\,000}$$
$$= 122\cdot5 \text{ Hz}$$

Exercises 3

1. A capacitor of 15 μF is connected in parallel with a coil of inductance 0·3 H and negligible resistance to a sinusoidal supply of 240V, 50 Hz. Calculate the resultant current and state whether the phase angle is a leading or lagging one.

2. Calculate the resulting supply current and the overall power factor when a resistor of 100Ω is connected in parallel with the circuit of question 1.

3. A coil of reactance 30Ω and resistance 40Ω is connected in parallel with a capacitor of reactance 200Ω and the circuit is supplied at 200V. Calculate the resultant current and power factor. Check the results by constructing the phasor diagram accurately to scale.

4. A parallel circuit consists of two branches. Branch A consists of a coil of resistance 100Ω and inductance 0·552 H. Branch B consists of a capacitor of 22·5 μF in series with a resistor of 141·4Ω. The supply to the circuit is 100V, 50 Hz. Determine (i) by graphical construction (ii) by calculation the resultant supply current and the overall power factor.

5. Calculate the values of the components which when connected in series will form a circuit equivalent to that of question 4.

6. A resistor of 12 ohms and a capacitor of 300 microfarads are connected in series. An inductive coil of inductance 0·5 henry and resistance 8 ohms is connected in parallel with the above. A single-phase supply at 240V, 50 Hz, is connected across the ends of the combination.

   Determine graphically or by calculation,
   - (a) the current and its power factor in each of the parallel circuits;
   - (b) the total current from the supply and its power factor.

7. A coil has resistance 150 Ω and inductance 0·478 H. Calculate the value of a capacitor which when connected in parallel with this coil to a 50-Hz supply will cause the resultant supply current to be in phase with the voltage.

8. The two branches of a parallel circuit consist respectively of a coil of inductance 0·636 H and resistance 300 Ω and a capacitor of 3 μF. Determine the frequency at which the supply voltage and current will be in phase.

9. An inductive coil of resistance 50 Ω takes a current of 1A when connected in series with a capacitor of 31·8 μF to a 240-V 50-Hz supply. Calculate the resultant supply current when the capacitor is connected in parallel with the coil to the same supply.

10. A coil of resistance 50 Ω and inductance 0·276 H is connected to a sinusoidal supply at 240V, 50 Hz. Calculate or determine graphically the value of a capacitor in microfarad which when connected in parallel with the coil will cause no change in the value of the supply current or overall power factor.

THREE-PHASE CIRCUIT CALCULATIONS I
STAR CONNECTIONS

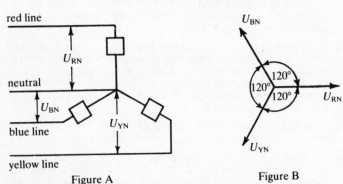

Figure A   Figure B

Figure A shows three loads connected in the star formation to a three-phase four-wire supply system. Figure B shows the phasor diagram, the red line to neutral voltage U_{RN} is taken as reference, the phase sequence is Red, Yellow, Blue so that the other line to neutral voltages (or *phase* voltages) lie as shown.

If $U_{RN} = U_{YN} = U_{BN}$ and they are equally spaced the system of *voltages* is balanced.

Let U_L be the voltage between any pair of lines (the *line* voltage) and

$$U_P = U_{RN} = U_{YN} = U_{BN} \quad \text{(the \textit{phase} voltage)}$$

Then $\qquad U_L = \sqrt{3}U_P$

and $\qquad I_L = I_P$

where I_L is the current in any line and I_P is the current in any load or phase. The power per phase is $P = U_P I_P \cos \phi$ and the total power is the sum of the amounts of power in each phase.

If the currents are equal and the phase angles are the same, as in figure C, the load on the system is balanced, the current in the neutral is zero and the total power is

$$P = \sqrt{3}\, U_L I_L \cos \phi$$

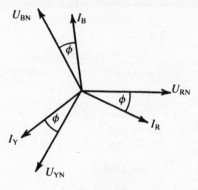

Figure C

Example

The following loads are connected to a 415-V three-phase four-wire system:

between red line and neutral, a non-inductive resistor of 24Ω;

between yellow line and neutral, 886W at 0·555 p.f. lagging;

between blue line and neutral, a capacitor of reactance 30Ω in series with a resistor of 40Ω.

The phase sequence is red, yellow, blue. Calculate:
  (*a*) the current in each line;
  (*b*) the total power;
  (*c*) the current in the neutral.

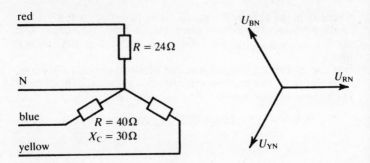

Line current = phase current

$$= \frac{\text{line to neutral voltage}}{\text{impedance between line and neutral}}$$

line to neutral voltage $= U_P = \dfrac{1}{\sqrt{3}} \times U_L$

$$= \frac{415}{\sqrt{3}}$$

$$= 240\text{V}$$

Current in red line $I_R = \dfrac{240}{24}$

$$= \underline{10\text{A}} \qquad\qquad (a)$$

The power in the yellow phase circuit

$$P_Y = U_{YN}I_Y \cos \phi_Y$$
$$886 = 240 \times I_Y \times 0.555$$

Current in yellow line

$$I_Y = \frac{886}{240 \times 0.555}$$

$$= \underline{6.65\text{A}} \qquad (a)$$

the phase angle between this current and the yellow to neutral voltage is given by

$$\cos \phi_Y = 0.555$$

$$\phi_Y = 56° \, 17' \quad \text{(lag)}$$

Current in the blue line

$$I_B = \frac{240}{\sqrt{(R^2 + X_C{}^2)}}$$

$$= \frac{240}{\sqrt{(40^2 + 30^2)}}$$

$$= \underline{4.8\text{A}} \qquad (a)$$

The phase angle between this current and the blue to neutral voltage is given by

$$\tan \phi_B = \frac{X_C}{R} = \frac{30}{40}$$

$$= 0.75$$

$$\phi_B = 36° \, 52' \quad \text{(lead)}$$

Power in the red phase $\quad P_R = 240 \times 10$
$$= 2400\text{W}$$

Power in the blue phase $P_B = 240 \times 4.8 \times \cos 36° \, 52'$
$$= 240 \times 4.8 \times 0.8$$
$$= 921.6\text{W}$$

Total power $\qquad P = 2400 + 886 + 921.6$
$$= \underline{4208\text{W}} \qquad (b)$$

To determine the neutral current graphically draw the phasor diagram of currents accurately to scale:

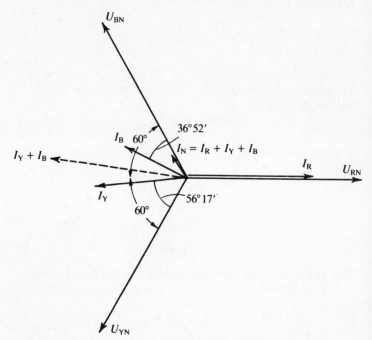

Note:

$$I_N = I_R + I_Y + I_B$$

means that I_N is the PHASOR sum of I_R, I_Y and I_B.

The phasors representing I_Y and I_B are first combined by completing the parallelogram. Their resultant is combined with phasor I_R to give the neutral current I_N which is determined by measurement.

Alternatively the neutral current may be calculated as follows:

Horizontal component of I_R = 10

Horizontal component of I_Y = $-6.65 \cos (60° - 56° \, 17')$

                                       = $-6.65 \cos 3° \, 43'$

                                       = $-6.65 \times 0.9979 = -6.636$

Horizontal component of I_B $= -4\cdot8 \cos (60° - 36° \, 52')$
$= -4\cdot8 \cos 23° \, 8'$
$= -4\cdot8 \times 0\cdot9196 = -4\cdot414$

Total horizontal component $X = 10 - 6\cdot636 - 4\cdot414$
$= -1\cdot05$

Vertical component of I_R $= 0$

Vertical component of I_Y $= -6\cdot65 \sin 3° \, 43'$
$= -6\cdot65 \times 0\cdot0648 = -0\cdot4309$

Vertical component of I_B $= 4\cdot8 \sin 23° \, 8'$
$= 4\cdot8 \times 0\cdot3928 = 1\cdot885$

Total vertical component Y $= 1\cdot885 - 0\cdot4309$
$= 1\cdot4541$

The neutral current I_N $= \sqrt{(X^2 + Y^2)}$
$= \sqrt{((1\cdot05)^2 + (1\cdot454)^2)}$
$= \underline{1\cdot798\text{A}}$

Remember that horizontal components are negative if they lie to the left of the origin 0. Vertical components are negative if they lie beneath the origin 0.

Exercises 4

1. Three equal coils of inductive reactance 30Ω and resistance 40Ω are connected in star to a three-phase supply of line voltage 400V. Calculate the line current and the total power.

2. The load connected between each line and the neutral of a 415-V, 50-Hz three-phase circuit consists of a capacitor of $31\cdot8\,\mu\text{F}$ in series with a resistor of 100Ω. Calculate the line current and the total power.

3. The load connected between each line and the neutral of a 415-V three-phase supply consists of:
   between red line and neutral, non-inductive resistance of 25Ω;
   between yellow line and neutral, inductive reactance 12Ω in series with resistance 5Ω;
   between blue line and neutral, capacitive reactance 17·3Ω in series with resistance 10Ω.
   Calculate the current in each line and the total power.

4. A star-connected resistance bank, each resistor of 30Ω is connected to a 415-V three-phase supply. Connected to the same supply is a star-connected capacitor bank, each capacitor having reactance 40Ω. Calculate the resultant current in each line and the total power.

5. The load connected between each line and neutral of a 415-V three-phase supply system consists of:

   between red line and neutral, 40 ohms resistance;

   between yellow line and neutral, 20 ohms resistance;

   between blue line and neutral, 60 ohms resistance.

   Calculate the current in the neutral, check the result by means of an accurately constructed phasor diagram. Calculate also the total power supplied.   (C & G)

6. A 415-V, 3-phase, 4-wire system supplies power to three non-inductive loads. The loads are 25 kW between red and neutral, 30 kW between yellow and neutral, and 12 kW between blue and neutral.
   Calculate (a) the current in each line wire, and (b) the current in the neutral conductor.   (C & G)

7. The load connected between each line and neutral of a 415-V three-phase four-wire system is as follows:

   red line   12 kW 0·866 p.f. lagging
   yellow line   10 kW unity p.f.
   blue line   8 kW 0·707 p.f. leading

   Determine graphically or by calculation the current in the neutral.

8. The load connected between each line and the neutral of a 415-V supply system consists of:

   between red line and neutral, 100Ω non inductive resistance;

   between yellow line and neutral, 100Ω inductive reactance;

   between blue line and neutral 100Ω capacitive reactance.

   The phase sequence is RYB. Calculate the current in the neutral.

9. Use a graphical construction to determine the neutral current of question 8 when the phase sequence is reversed.

10. The circuit shown overleaf is connected to a 415-V 50-Hz supply with phase sequence RYB. Calculate or determine graphically the current in the neutral.

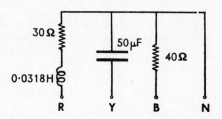

THREE-PHASE CIRCUIT CALCULATIONS II
DELTA CONNECTIONS

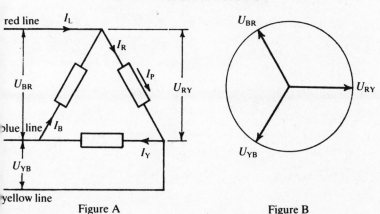

Figure A

Figure B

Figure A shows three loads connected in the delta or mesh formation to a three-phase supply system. Figure B shows the phasor diagram of the line voltages with the red to yellow voltage taken as reference.

The voltage applied to any load is the line voltage U_L and the line current is the phasor difference between the currents in the two loads connected to that line. In particular if the load currents are all equal and make equal phase angles with their respective voltages the system is balanced and

$$I_L = \sqrt{3}I_P$$

The total power under these conditions is

$$P = \sqrt{3}U_L I_L \cos \phi$$

47

Example

Three coils each of resistance 40Ω and inductive reactance 30Ω are connected in delta to a 400-V three-phase system.

Calculate:

(a) the current in each coil,
(b) the line current,
(c) the total power.

The circuit diagram is as figure A.

Impedance of each coil $Z = \sqrt{R^2 + X_L^2}$

$$= \sqrt{40^2 + 30^2}$$

$$= 50\Omega$$

Current in each coil $\quad = \dfrac{U}{Z}$

$$= \frac{400}{50} = \underline{8A} \qquad (a)$$

line current $\quad I_L = \sqrt{3} \times 8$

$$= \underline{13 \cdot 86A} \qquad (b)$$

The power factor of the coil is

$$\cos \phi = \frac{R}{Z}$$

$$= \frac{40}{50}$$

$$= 0 \cdot 8$$

The total power $\quad P = \sqrt{3} U_L I_L \cos \phi$

$$= \sqrt{3} \times 400 \times 13 \cdot 86 \times 0 \cdot 8$$

$$= \underline{7682W} \qquad (c)$$

Exercises 5

1. Three resistors each of 30Ω are connected

   (a) in star,
   (b) in delta,

   to a 415-V three-phase system. Calculate the current in each resistor, the line current and the total power for each connection.

2. Each branch of a mesh-connected load consists of resistance 20Ω in series with inductive reactance 30Ω. The line voltage is 400V. Calculate the line current and the total power.

3. Three coils each with resistance 45Ω and with inductance 0·2 H, are connected to a 415-V, 3-phase supply at 50 Hz

   (a) in mesh, (b) in star.

   Calculate for each method of connection

   (i) the current in each coil, and
   (ii) the total power in the circuit.   (C & G)

4. A three-phase load consists of three similar inductive coils, each of resistance 50Ω and inductance 0·3 H. The supply is 415V, 50 Hz.

   Calculate:

   (a) the line current;
   (b) the power factor;
   (c) the total power;

   when the load is (i) star-connected, (ii) delta-connected.

                                                           (C & G)

5. Three equal resistors are required to absorb a total of 24 kW from a 415-V three-phase system. Calculate the value of each resistor when they are connected

   (a) in star, (b) in mesh.

6. To improve the power factor of a certain installation requires a total of 48 kVAr equally distributed over the three phases of a 415-V 50-Hz system. Calculate the value of the capacitors required (in microfarads) when the capacitors are connected

   (a) in star, (b) in delta.

7. The following loads are connected to a three-phase three-wire 415-V 50-Hz supply system:

   between red and yellow lines non-inductive resistance 60Ω;
   between yellow and blue lines a coil of inductive reactance 30Ω and resistance 40Ω;
   between blue and red lines a capacitor of 100 μF.

   Calculate the current through each load and the total power.

49

8. A 415-V 3-phase star-connected alternator supplies a delta-connected induction motor of full load efficiency 87% and power factor 0·8 which delivers 14 920W. Calculate:

    (a) current in each motor winding;

    (b) current in each alternator winding;

    (c) the power to be developed by the engine driving the alternator assuming that the efficiency of the alternator is 82%.

THREE-PHASE POWER AND POWER FACTOR IMPROVEMENT

References: **Watts.**

                Voltamperes.

                Reactive voltamperes.

                Tariffs.

Examples

A.   A works load consists of

      (i) 9 kW of lighting at unity p.f.;

      (ii) a motor taking 12 kVA at 0·75 p.f. lagging;

      (iii) a number of small motors taking 15 kW at 0·6 p.f. lagging.

The loads are balanced over the three phases of a 415-V supply system. Determine:

    (a) the total kW;

    (b) the total kVAr;

    (c) the overall kVA;

    (d) the overall power factor;

    (e) the line current.

The power triangle for a lagging power factor load is as shown in volume 2 thus:

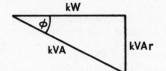

cos ϕ is the power actor.

50

For load (ii) 12 kVA at 0·75 p.f. lagging:

$\cos \phi = 0.75$, $\phi = 41° 24'$ $\sin \phi = 0.6613$

true power   = kVA × power factor
                    = 12 × 0·75
                    = 9 kW

Reactive kVAr = kVA $\sin \phi$
                    = 12 × 0·6613
                    = 7·9356
                    = 7·936

For load (iii) $\cos \phi = 0.6$, $\phi = 53° 8'$, $\tan \phi = 1.3335$

$$\frac{kVAr}{kW} = \tan \phi$$

kVAr = kW $\tan \phi$
        = 15 × 1·3335
        = 20

These results may then be tabulated

Load	kW	kVAr	
i	9	0	
ii	9	7·936	
iii	15	20	
Total	33	27·936	*(a)* *(b)*

Note: only kW and kVAr may be added directly.

The combined load is then represented by a power triangle drawn to scale if required.

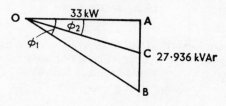

51

Overall kVA $= \sqrt{33^2 + 27{\cdot}936^2}$ (or by measurement)

$= \underline{43{\cdot}23 \text{ kVA}}$ (c)

The overall power factor

$$\cos \phi_1 = \frac{\text{kW}}{\text{kVA}}$$

$$= \frac{33}{43{\cdot}23}$$

$$= \underline{0{\cdot}763} \quad \text{lag} \qquad (d)$$

since $VA = \sqrt{3} U_L I_L$ in a three-phase system

the line current $I_L = \dfrac{VA}{\sqrt{3} \times U_L}$

$$= \frac{43{\cdot}23 \times 1000}{\sqrt{3} \times 415}$$

$$= \underline{60{\cdot}1\text{A}} \qquad (e)$$

Note: The calculations may also be performed on a single-phase basis if desired but since the loads are balanced this is not really necessary.

B. Calculate:

(a) the total kVAr to be supplied by a capacitor bank in order to improve the overall power factor of the system of example A to 0·9 p.f. lagging;

(b) The value of capacitance required assuming that the capacitors are connected (i) in star, (ii) in delta.

Using the accurately drawn power triangle of the previous example and inserting the additional line OC set off from OA at an angle ϕ_2 given by

$$\cos \phi_2 = 0{\cdot}9$$

$$\phi_2 = 25° \; 50'$$

BC represents the leading kVAr required to bring about the desired improvement. The kVAr may be found by measuring BC or by calculation as follows:

$$BC = AB - AC$$

as previously determined

$$AB = 27 \cdot 936$$

similarly

$$AC = 33 \tan 25° \, 50'$$
$$= 33 \times 0 \cdot 4841$$
$$= 15 \cdot 97$$
$$BC = 27 \cdot 936 - 15 \cdot 97$$
$$= \underline{11 \cdot 966} \qquad (a)$$

this is the total kVAr required.

kVAr required per phase

$$= \frac{11 \cdot 966}{3}$$
$$= 3 \cdot 989 \text{ or } 3989 \text{ VAr}$$

since in a capacitive circuit

$$I = \frac{U}{X_C}$$

multiply both sides by V so that

$$UI = \frac{U^2}{X_C} \quad \text{(volt ampères reactive)}$$

Thus

$$\frac{U^2}{X_C} = 3989$$

For the star connection $U = \dfrac{1}{\sqrt{3}} \times 415$

$$= 240 \text{V}$$

and

$$\frac{240^2}{X_C} = 3989$$
$$X_C = \frac{240^2}{3989}$$
$$= 14 \cdot 44 \, \Omega$$
$$\frac{10^6}{2\pi f C} = 14 \cdot 44$$

53

$$C = \frac{10^6}{2\pi \times 50 \times 14 \cdot 44}$$

$$= \underline{220 \ \mu F}$$

so that three capacitors each of 220 μF connected in star would be required. (b) (i).

For the delta connection $U = 415$V

and

$$\frac{415^2}{X_C} = 3989$$

$$X_C = \frac{415^2}{3989}$$

$$= 43 \cdot 16 \Omega$$

$$C = \frac{10^6}{2\pi \times 50 \times 43 \cdot 16}$$

$$= \underline{73 \cdot 7 \ \mu F}$$

so that three capacitors each of 73·7 μF connected in delta would be required. (b) (ii).

C. Calculate the cost per year of the energy supplied to a factory which is loaded daily as follows: 250 kVA for 2 hours; 180 kVA for 8 hours, and 75 kVA for 6 hours per day. The charge for the energy is made on the basis of £26 per kVA of maximum demand plus 5·8p per unit.

Maximum demand = 250 kVA
Maximum demand charge = 250 × £26 = £6 500.

Assuming a 5-day week and 50-week year the total number of units consumed in one year is

$$250 \times 2 \times 5 \times 50 = 125 \ 000$$
$$+ \ 180 \times 8 \times 5 \times 50 = 360 \ 000$$
$$+ \ 75 \times 6 \times 5 \times 50 = \underline{112 \ 500}$$

Total $\qquad$ 597 500

54

Annual cost of units = 597 500 × 5·8p
= 3 465 500p
= £34655·00
Total annual cost = £6500 + £34655
= £41155

D. Calculate the annual cost of the energy supplied to the installation of example C if additionally there is a power factor penalty clause which allows for the cost per kVA of maximum demand to be increased by £1·90 for every 0·1 by which the power factor falls below 0·85 and the average power factor is 0·7.

Determine also the overall cost per unit under these conditions.

Additional cost per kVA of maximum demand.

$$= \frac{(0·85 - 0·7)}{0·1} \times £1·90$$

$$= \frac{0·15}{0·1} \times £1·90$$

$$= £2·85$$

New maximum demand charge = 250 × £28·85
= £7212·50

Total annual cost = £7212·50 + £34655 = £41867·50

$$\text{Overall cost per unit} = \frac{£41867·50}{597\ 500}$$

$$= \frac{4\ 186\ 750}{597\ 500}\text{p}$$

$$= 7\text{p}$$

Exercises 6

1. An installation supplies the following loads:
   (i) 10 kW at unity power factor;
   (ii) 15 kVA at 0·8 p.f. lagging;
   (iii) 4 kVAr leading.
   Calculate the total kW, kVAr, the overall kVA and power factor.

2. The following loads are balanced over the three phases of a 415-V supply system:
    (i) 20 kVA at 0·8 p.f. lagging;
    (ii) 25 kVA at 0·6 p.f. lagging;
    (iii) 30 kW at unity p.f.

    Calculate the overall power factor and the line current.

3. (a) Calculate the line current taken by a 415-V, 3-phase motor working at full load output of 14 920W when its efficiency is 85% and power factor 0·7.
   (b) Determine the line current and resultant power factor when a capacitor bank of 8 kVAr is connected in parallel with the motor.

4. A 415-V three-phase system supplies the following balanced loads:
    (i) 8 kW of lighting at unity power factor;
    (ii) a motor of full load efficiency 80%, power output 7460W and power factor 0·75 lagging;
    (iii) a number of small motors of output totalling 8952W, efficiency 70% and power factor 0·7 lagging.

    Determine the total load in kW, kVAr, and kVA, the overall power factor and the line current.

5. Determine:
   (a) the total leading kVAr required to improve the power factor of question 4 to 0·9 lagging;
   (b) the values of capacitors (in microfarads) required to supply the kVAr if the capacitors are connected (i) in star, (ii) in delta. (Supply frequency 50 Hz.)

6. The load in a small works consists of 20 kW at unity power-factor, and a number of small single-phase motors of output totalling 44 760W, working at 86 per cent efficiency and at a power-factor of 0·7 lagging.

   Find, graphically or by calculation:
   (a) the combined load in kVA;
   (b) the overall power-factor;
   (c) the load in kW;
   (d) the total current taken from a 240-V single-phase supply.
   (C & G)

7. A consumer is supplied with electric power at 415V, 3-phase, 4-wire. The total load consists of:
   (a) 50 kW for heating and lighting at unity power-factor;

56

(b) 90 kVA of induction motors at 0·7 power-factor lagging;

(c) 30 kVA to a rotary convertor at 0·6 power-factor leading;
each of these loads being balanced across the three phases.

Find the value of the line current, and the power-factor of the combined load. (C & G)

8. Explain the meaning of power-factor, and use a phasor diagram to illustrate power-factor improvement.

The power taken by a 415-V, 50-Hz, 3-phase induction motor is 60 kW at 0·75 power-factor lagging. A bank of capacitors is connected in delta across the supply lines to improve the overall power-factor.

Calculate the capacitance per phase and the total capacitance required to raise the power-factor to 0·9 lagging. (C & G)

9. (a) The power supply to a 415-V, 50-Hz, 3-phase induction motor is 50 kW at 0·72 power-factor lagging. A bank of capacitors is connected in mesh across the supply lines to improve the overall power-factor.

Calculate the capacitance per phase in order to raise the power-factor to 0·9 lagging.

(b) Describe briefly a different method of power-factor improvement which could be used in a large works to improve the overall power-factor. (C & G)

10. Complete the table which refers to the loads supplied by a 3-phase 415-V system. Each load is balanced over the three phases.

Load	kVA	kW	kVAr	power factor	line current
a	15	12			(lag)
b		12		1·0	
c		0	8		(lead)
d				0·8 lag	20

Overall values.

11. (a) Explain with connection diagram how two single-phase wattmeters may be used to measure the power supply to a three-phase load.

(b) The steady readings on two such wattmeters are 14 kW and 35 kW. Calculate:

(i) the power in kW taken by the load;

(ii) the power factor;

(iii) the load in kVA, and

(iv) the line current, if the supply is at 415V, three-phase

57

(c) What assumptions would be made if ONE single-phase wattmeter only were to be used? Show, with a diagram, how the instrument would be connected.

12. The cost of electrical power to a consumer is £25·60 per annum per kVA of maximum demand, plus 5·5p per unit.

A consumer's maximum demand is 450 kW at 0·72 power-factor lagging, and his annual consumption is 720 000 kWh.

   (a) Calculate the overall cost per unit.
   (b) Describe, giving reasons, one method by which the consumer could reduce the cost of his power whilst taking the same number of units.

13. (a) A consumer has a lighting load of 3·6 kW, and is to install some electric heaters. The following alternative tariffs are available:

Two part: £10·05 per quarter, plus 6·9p per unit for all units consumed.

Flat rate: 11·29p per unit for lighting and 6·46p for heating.

Assuming that all the apparatus will have an average use of 4 hours daily throughout the year, calculate the kW rating of the proposed electric heaters, so that the annual cost of electricity on each tariff shall be equal.

   (b) A large industrial consumer pays for energy under the following tariff:

£27·60 per annum per kVA of maximum demand plus 6·3p per unit.

Explain briefly why this tariff is used.

14. (a) Justify the general use of two-part tariffs in electricity supply. Give details of one form of domestic two-part tariff.

   (b) A power consumer with a constant maximum demand throughout the year, is offered the following tariff: £27·05 per kW of maximum demand per annum plus 4·6p per unit. The tariff also includes a power factor clause to the effect that "the amount payable for each kW of maximum demand shall be increased by 1% for each 0·01 by which the average lagging power-factor is less than 0·9." The annual maximum demand is 300 kW, the average power-factor is 0·7 lagging, and the annual consumption is 600 000 units. Calculate:

      (i) the annual cost and cost per unit, when the power-factor remains at 0·7 lagging.
      (ii) the annual cost and cost per unit, if the average power-factor were improved to 0·9 lagging.

VOLTAGE DROP CALCULATIONS IN THREE-PHASE CIRCUITS

References: **Resistance of conductors.**
Regulations for The Electrical Equipment of Buildings (IEE).

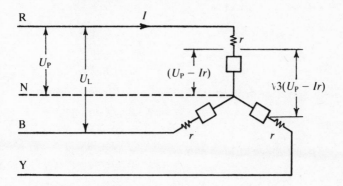

Consider a balanced load connected to a three-phase system as shown so that the line current is I ampere. Each core of the cable is assumed to have resistance r ohm and negligible reactance. The cable resistance is shown in series with each leg of the load.

Let phase and line voltages at the supply end be U_P and U_L respectively. The voltage drop in each line is Ir and, if the cable reactance and the load power factor are ignored, the phase voltage at the load end is $U_P - Ir$.

The line voltage at the supply end is $U_L = \sqrt{3}\, U_P$ and the line voltage at the load end is

$$\sqrt{3} \times \text{phase voltage} = \sqrt{3}\,(U_P - Ir)$$
$$= \sqrt{3}\, U_P - \sqrt{3}\, Ir$$
$$= U_L - \sqrt{3}\, Ir$$

Thus the voltage drop referred to the line voltage or total voltage drop is $\sqrt{3}Ir$.

Examples

A. A balanced load of 35A is supplied over a distance of 250 m through a cable each core of which has resistance 1·351Ω per 1000 m. The line voltage at the supply end is 415V. Calculate the line voltage at the load end and determine the percentage drop in the line voltage.

$$\text{Resistance per core} = \frac{250}{1000} \times 1\cdot351$$

$$= 0\cdot3378\Omega$$

$$\text{voltage drop per core} = 35 \times 0\cdot3378$$

$$= 11\cdot823V$$

equivalent drop in the line voltage (the *total* drop)

$$= \sqrt{3} \times 11\cdot823$$

$$= 20\cdot48V$$

$$\text{line voltage at load end} = 415 - 20\cdot48$$

$$= \underline{394\cdot5V}$$

$$\text{percentage drop in line voltage} = \frac{20\cdot48}{415} \times 100$$

$$= \underline{4\cdot93\%}$$

B. A three-phase 10-kW motor operates on full load with efficiency 80% and power factor 0·75. It is supplied from a switchboard through a cable each core of which has resistance 0·2Ω. Calculate the voltage necessary at the supply end in order that the voltage at the load end terminals shall be 415V.

The full load current of the motor is

$$I = \frac{10 \times 1000}{\sqrt{(3)} \times 415 \times 0\cdot75} \times \frac{100}{80}$$

$$= 23\cdot19A$$

The voltage drop per core of the cable

$$= 23\cdot19 \times 0\cdot2$$

$$= 4\cdot638V$$

The equivalent reduction in the line voltage

$$= \sqrt{3} \times 4{\cdot}638$$
$$= 8{\cdot}03V$$

The required line voltage at the switchboard

$$= 415 + 8{\cdot}03$$
$$= \underline{423V}$$

This is not a rigid treatment of the problem but the method gives a result sufficiently accurate for most practical purposes.

C. The estimated load in a factory extension is 50 kW balanced at 0·8 p.f. The supply point is 120 metres away and the supply voltage is 415V. Calculate the cross-sectional area of the cable in order that the total voltage drop shall not exceed 2·5% of the supply voltage.

Take the resistivity of copper as $1{\cdot}78 \times 10^{-8}\Omega$m

The line current

$$I = \frac{50 \times 1000}{\sqrt{(3)} \times 415 \times 0{\cdot}8}$$
$$= 86{\cdot}95A$$

Allowable reduction in line voltage

$$= 2{\cdot}5\% \times 415$$
$$= 10{\cdot}375V$$

Equivalent reduction in phase voltage

$$= \frac{10{\cdot}375}{\sqrt{3}}$$
$$= 5{\cdot}99V$$

Resistance per core of the cable

$$= \frac{5{\cdot}99}{86{\cdot}95}$$
$$= 0{\cdot}0689\Omega$$

The resistance of a cable is given by

$$R = \frac{\rho l}{A}$$

where ρ is the resistivity (Ωm)
l is the length (m)
A is the cross-sectional
area (m^2)

so that

$$A = \frac{\rho l}{R}$$

$$A = \frac{1 \cdot 78 \Omega\text{m} \times 120 \text{ m}}{10^8 \times 0 \cdot 0689 \Omega}$$

$$= \frac{0 \cdot 31}{10^4} \text{ m}^2$$

$$= \frac{0 \cdot 31}{10^4} \text{m}^2 \left[\frac{10^6 \text{ mm}^2}{1 \text{ m}^2} \right]$$

$$= 31 \text{ mm}^2$$

D. The nearest standard size cable to that required for example C is 35 mm^2. Calculate the actual voltage drop using this cable and the line voltage at the load end.

We notice that the resistance of a cable is inversely proportional to its cross-sectional area, i.e.

$$R \propto \frac{1}{A}$$

and also that the voltage drop for a given current is directly proportional to the resistance,

i.e. $\qquad U \propto R$

so that $\qquad U \propto R \propto \dfrac{1}{A}$

or $\qquad U \propto \dfrac{1}{A}$

Thus if U_2 is the voltage drop when the area is A_2 and U_1 is the voltage drop when the area is A_1

then $\qquad U_2 \propto \dfrac{1}{A_2}$ or $U_2 = \dfrac{k}{A_2}$

and $\qquad U_1 \propto \dfrac{1}{A_1}$ or $U_1 = \dfrac{k}{A_1}$ where k is a constant.

Dividing we have

$$\frac{U_2}{U_1} = \frac{A_1}{A_2} \quad k \text{ cancelling.}$$

Let $U_1 = 5 \cdot 99$ when $A_1 = 31$ mm^2 as calculated and U_2 is the new voltage drop when $A_2 = 35$ mm^2

$$\frac{U_2}{5 \cdot 99} = \frac{31}{35}$$

$$U_2 = 5 \cdot 99 \times \frac{31}{35}$$

$$= \underline{5 \cdot 305 \text{V}}$$

The line voltage at the load end

$$= 415 - \sqrt{3} \times 5 \cdot 305$$

$$= 415 - 9 \cdot 19$$

$$= 405 \cdot 81$$

$$\text{or} \quad \underline{406 \text{V}}$$

Again, this is not a rigid treatment but the result is sufficiently accurate for many practical purposes.

E. A balanced three-phase load of 25A is supplied over a distance of 55 m through a 6-mm^2 mineral-insulated cable. The voltage drop for this cable is 6·8 mV per ampère per metre. Calculate the total voltage drop.

Total voltage drop

$$= 6 \cdot 8 \; \frac{\text{mV}}{\text{A.\cancel{m}}} \times 25 \cancel{\text{A}} \times 55 \cancel{\text{m}}$$

$$= 9350 \text{ mV}$$

$$\text{or} \quad \underline{9 \cdot 35 \text{V}}$$

F. A balanced load of 25A is to be supplied from the 415-V mains to a point 150 m away. The total voltage drop must not exceed 4% of the supply voltage. Choose the most suitable cable from those given below.

cable size (mm²)	6	10	16	25
current rating (A)	34	46	62	80
voltage drop per ampère per metre (mV)	6·4	3·8	2·4	1·5

Permissible total voltage drop

$$= 4\cdot0\% \times 415$$
$$= 16\cdot6\text{V}$$

denoting the figures in the bottom line of the table by x we have

$$x\ \frac{\text{mV}}{\text{A.m}}\left[\frac{1\text{V}}{1000\ \text{mV}}\right] \times 25\text{A} \times 150\ \text{m} \leqslant 16\cdot6$$

$$\frac{x \times 25 \times 150}{1000} \leqslant 16\cdot6\ (\leqslant \text{means less than})$$

$$x \leqslant \frac{16\cdot6 \times 1000}{25 \times 150}$$

$$\leqslant 4\cdot43$$

so we choose a figure in the bottom line of the table which is less than 4·43

The appropriate size of cable is thus 10 mm².

The procedure then, is to choose a cable having a voltage drop figure which is less than

$$\frac{\text{permissible voltage drop} \times 1000}{\text{current required} \times \text{length of run (metres)}}$$

For the following examples reference to the 16th Edition of the IEE Wiring Regulations and the IEE On-Site Guide will be necessary.

G. A p.v.c. trunking is to be used to enclose single-core p.v.c.-insulated distribution cables (copper conductors) for a distance of 30m from the main switchgear of an office building to supply a new 415 V T.P. and N distribution fuseboard. The balanced load consists of 24kW of discharge lighting. The fuses at the main switch-fuse and at the distribution board are to BS 88 part 2. The voltage drop in the cables must not exceed 6V. The ambient temperature is anticipated to be 35°C. The declared value of I_p is 20kA and that of Z_e is 0·30. Assume that the requirements of Regulation 434-03 are satisfied by the use of BS 88 fuses.

a) For the distribution cables, establish the:
   i) design current (I_b)
   ii) minimum rating of fuse in the main switch fuse (I_n)
   iii) maximum mV/A/m value
   iv) minimum current rating (I_t)
   v) minimum cross-sectional area of the live conductors
   vi) actual voltage drop in the cables

b) It is proposed to install a 2·5mm² protective conductor within the p.v.c. trunking. Verify that this meets shock protection requirements. (C & G)

a) i) Design current $I_b = \dfrac{24 \times 10^3 \times 1·8}{\sqrt{3} \times 415}$ (1·8 factor for discharge lighting)

$= 60·1\text{A}$

ii) Minimum BS 88 fuse rating (I_n) is 63A

iii) Maximum mV/A/m value $= \dfrac{6 \times 1000}{60·1 \times 30}$

$= 3·33 \text{ mV/A/m}$

iv) Minimum current rating $(I_t) = \dfrac{63}{0·94}$ (temperature correction factor C_a for 35°C)

$= 67·02\text{A}$

v) Minimum c.s.a. of cable is 16mm² (68A 2·4mV/A/m)

vi) Actual voltage drop in 30m = $\dfrac{2\cdot4 \times 60\cdot1 \times 30}{1000}$

$$= \quad 4\cdot33\text{V}$$

b) Check compliance with Table 41D (IEE Regulations) Using On-site Guide.
From Table 6A, $R_1 + R_2$ for 16mm²/2·5mm² = 1·15 + 7·41 mΩ/m
From Table 6B, factor of 1·38 must be applied
Now $Z_s = Z_e + R_1 + R_2$
$R_1 + R_2 = \dfrac{30 \times (1\cdot15 + 7\cdot41) \times 1\cdot38}{1000}$

$$\begin{aligned}
&= \quad 0\cdot354\Omega \\
\therefore Z_s &= \quad 0\cdot3 + 0\cdot354 \\
Z_s &= \quad 0\cdot654\Omega
\end{aligned}$$

This satisfies table 41D as the maximum Z_s for a 63A fuse is 0·86Ω

H. It is proposed to install a new 240 V 50Hz distribution board in a factory kitchen some 40 m distant from the supplier's intake position.

It is to be supplied by two 25 mm² p.v.c. insulated cables (copper conductors) single-core cables in steel conduit. Protection at origin of the cables is to be by BS 88 fuses rated at 80A.

It is necessary for contractual purposes to establish:
a) the prospective short circuit current (p.s.c.c) at the distribution board, and
b) that the proposed distribution cables will comply with IEE Regulation 434-03-03.

A test conducted at the intake position between phase and neutral to determine the external impedance of the suppliers system indicates a value of 0·012 Ω.

a) The resistance of distribution cables from intake to distribution board

From Table 6A (On-Site Guide), R_1/R_2 for 25 mm cables = 1·454 mV/m

From Table 6B a multiplier of 1·38 is necessary using the Table 6A figures as $R_1/R_2 = \dfrac{40 \times 1\cdot454 \times 1\cdot38}{1000}$

$$= 0\cdot08 \; \Omega \text{ (regard this as impedance)}$$

So total short circuit fault impedance = 0·12 + 0·08

$$= 0\cdot2 \; \Omega$$

Thus
$$I_f = \frac{240}{0\cdot2}$$
$$\therefore \text{ p.s.c.c} = 1200\text{A}$$

From Appendix 3 fig 3A the BS88 fuse clearance time is approximately 0·12s

b) From Regulation 434-03-03 $t = \dfrac{k^2 \; S^2}{I^2}$

$$= \frac{115^2 \times 25^2}{1200^2}$$

$\therefore$ limiting time for conductors (t) = 5·74 s

The cables are disconnected well before the 25 mm² cable conductors reach their limiting temperature, thus they are protected thermally.

I. Two 25mm² single-core p.v.c. insulated cables (COPPER CONDUCTORS) are drawn into a p.v.c. conduit along with a 10 mm² protective conductor to feed a 240V industrial heater.

The following details are relevant:

Protection at the origin is by 80 A BS 88 fuses.

The tested value of Z_e at the cables origin is 0·4Ω

The length of cables run is 55 m.

a) Establish the:
   i) value of $R_1 + R_2$ of the cables
   ii) prospective earth fault loop current (I_{ef})
   iii) the clearance time of the fuse
b) Does the clearance time comply with IEE Regulations?

a) i) Using the IEE On-Site Guide
   From Table 6A $R_1 + R_2$ for 25 mm²/10 mm² cables
   = 2·557 mΩ/m
   From Table 6B apply the factor 1·38

   Thus $R_1 + R_2 = \dfrac{55 \times 2·557 \times 1·38}{1000}$
   = 0·194 Ω

   So Z_s at distribution board = 0·4 + 0·194
                                = 0·594 Ω

   ii) Prospective earth fault loop current $(I_{ef}) = \dfrac{240}{0·594}$
                                                     = 404A

   iii) Using the IEE Wiring Regulations
      From App. 3 Table 3A the fuse clearance time is 5s.

b) The clearance time complies with IEE Regulation 413-02-13 which specifies maximum clearance (disconnection) time of 5s

J. It is necessary to confirm that the cross-sectional area of the protective conductor in a previously installed 415/240 V distribution circuit complies with IEE Regulation 543-01-03. The phase conductors are 10 mm² and the circuit-protective conductor is 2·5 mm². The length of the cables run in plastic conduit is 85 m. Protection is by 32 A, BS 88 fuses and the value of Z_e is 0·4 Ω.

Using the IEE On-Site Guide
   From Table 6A $R_1 + R_2$ for 10 mm²/2·5 mm² cables = 1·83 + 7·41 mΩ/m

   From Table 6B apply the factor 1·38
   Thus $R_1 + R_2$ = $\dfrac{85 \times (1·83 + 7·41) \times 1·38}{1000}$

                   = 1·084 Ω

So Z_s at distribution board $= 0 \cdot 4 + 1 \cdot 084$
$$= 1 \cdot 484 \, \Omega$$

Prospective earth fault loop current $(I_{ef}) = \dfrac{240}{1 \cdot 484}$

$$= 162 \text{A}$$

Using the IEE Wiring Regulations
From App. 3 Table 3A the fuse clearance time is $0 \cdot 9$ s.

From IEE Regulation 543-01-03 $\quad s = \dfrac{\sqrt{I^2 t}}{k}$ (k is 115 Table 54C)

$$= \dfrac{\sqrt{1 \, 62^2 \times 0 \cdot 9}}{115}$$

$$= \underline{1 \cdot 34 \text{ mm}^2}$$

This confirms that a $2 \cdot 5$ mm^2 protective conductor is acceptable.

Exercises 7

1. A balanced load of 30A is supplied through a cable each core of which has resistance $0 \cdot 28\Omega$. The line voltage at the supply end is 415V. Calculate the voltage at the load end, the percentage total voltage drop and the power wasted in the cable.

2. Each core of a three-core cable, 164 m long, has a cross-sectional area of 35 mm^2. The cable supplies power to a 30-kW, 415-V, three-phase motor working at full load with 87% efficiency and power factor $0 \cdot 72$ lagging. Calculate:

   (a) the voltage required at the supply end of the cable;
   (b) the power loss in the cable.

   The resistivity of copper may be taken as $1 \cdot 78 \times 10^{-8} \Omega$m and the reactance of the cable may be neglected.

3. A 40-kW, 415-V, three-phase motor, running at full load, has efficiency 86% and power factor $0 \cdot 75$ lagging. The three-core

cable connecting the motor to the switchboard is 110 m long and its conductors are of copper 25 mm² in cross-section.

Calculate the total voltage drop in the cable, neglecting reactance.

If the cable runs underground for most of its length, choose a suitable type of cable for the purpose and give a descriptive sketch of the system of laying it.

The resistivity of copper may be taken as $1.78 \times 10^{-8} \Omega m$.

4. The estimated load in a factory extension is 200 kW at 0.85 p.f. (balanced). The supply point is 75 m away where the line voltage is 415V. Choose the most suitable size of cable from those given below in order that the total voltage drop shall not exceed 2.5% of supply voltage.

   Cross-sectional areas
   of available conductors (mm²)   35   50   70   95
   (Resistivity of conductor is $1.78 \times 10^{-8} \Omega m$)

5. A motor taking 200 kW at 0.76 p.f. is supplied at 415V three-phase by means of a three-core copper 200 m long.
   a) Calculate the minimum cable cross-sectional area if the voltage drop is not to exceed 5 V.
   b) If the cable size calculated is non-standard, select from the table a suitable standard cable and calculate the actual voltage drop using that cable.
   Standard cross-sectional areas of cable conductors (mm²)
   300   400   500   630
   (Resistivity of copper $1.78 \times 10^{-8} \Omega m$)

6. A three-phase current of 35A is supplied to a point 75 m away by a cable which produces a voltage drop of 2.2 mV per ampere per metre. Calculate the total voltage drop.

The following questions should be answered by reference to the appropriate tables in the IEE Wiring Regulations (16th edition 1991) and/or the IEE On-Site Guide to the Wiring Regulations

7. A balanced load of 85A is required at a point 250 m distant from a 415 V supply position. Choose a suitable cable (clipped direct) from tables 4E4A and 4E4B in order that the total voltage drop shall be within the IEE specified limit (ambient temperature 30°C)

8. A 25 kW, 415 V 3-phase motor having full load efficiency and power factor 80% and 0.85 respectively is supplied from a point

160 m away from the main switchboard. It is intended to employ a surface run, multicore p.v.c. – insulated cable, non-armoured (COPPER CONDUCTORS). The ambient temperature is 30°C and BS 88 fuses are to be employed at the main switchboard. Select a cable to satisfy the IEE requirements.

9. The total load on a factory sub-distribution board consists of:
   10 kW lighting balanced over three phases, unity power factor;
   50 kW heating balanced over three phases, unity power factor and
   30 kW motor load having an efficiency 80%, power factor 0·8.
   The line voltage is 415 V and the supply point is 130 m distant.
   Protection at the origin of the cable (clipped direct) is by BS 88 fuses
   The ambient temperature is 30°C.
   Select a suitable cable from tables 4D2A and 4D2B, in order that the voltage drop shall not exceed 3% of the supply voltage.

10. Calculate the additional load in amperes which could be supplied by the cable chosen for question 10 with the voltage drop remaining within the specified limits.

11. A 12kW, 415V 3 phase industrial heater is to be wired using single-core p.v.c. insulated cables (COPPER CONDUCTORS) 30 m in length drawn into a steel conduit. The following details may be relevant to your calculation:-
    Ambient temperature 40°C
    Protection by BS 3036 (semi-enclosed) fuses
    Voltage drop in the cables must not exceed 10V
    The contract document calls for a 2·5 mm² conductor to be drawn into the conduit as a supplementary protective conductor.
    The worst section of the conduit run involves two right angle bends in 7 m. Establish the:
    a) design current (I_b)
    b) minimum fuse rating (I_n)
    c) maximum mV/A/m value
    d) minimum live cable rating (I_t)
    e) minimum live cable c.s.a.
    f) actual voltage drop.
    g) minimum conduit size.

12. The external live conductor impedance and external earth fault loop impedance are tested at the intake of a 240 V single phase installation and show values of 0·14 Ω and 0·28 Ω respectively. A

p.v.c. trunking runs from the intake position to a distribution board 40 m distant and contains 35 mm² live conductors and a 10 mm² protective conductor.

a) Estimate the:
   i) prospective short circuit current (p.s.s.c) at the distribution board
   ii) p.s.s.c. clearance time of the 100A BS 88 fuse at the origin of the cable
   iii) value of the earth fault loop impedance (Z_s) at the distribution board
   iv) prospective earth fault loop current
   v) earth fault clearance time of the BS 88 fuse at the origin of the cable
b) State the maximum permitted value of Z_s under these conditions

ELECTROMAGNETISM I

References: **Magnetic flux and flux density.**
Magnetising force.
Permeability and relative permeability.
Series and parallel magnetic circuits.

Magnetising Force (H)

To find the magnetising force of a coil having N turns and carrying a current I ampère when it is wound on a magnetic circuit of mean length l m.

$$H = \frac{I \times N}{l} \text{ ampère turns per metre (At/m)}$$

The product $I \times N$ is called the **magnetomotive force** (m.m.f.) of the coil.

Examples

A. Determine the magnetising force of a coil of 100 turns, carrying a current of three ampères, on a magnetic circuit 150 mm long.

$$H = \frac{I \times N}{l}$$

72

$$= \frac{3 \times 100}{150/1000}$$

(Note conversion of 150 mm
to metres)

$$= \frac{3 \times 100 \times 1000}{150}$$

$$= \underline{2000 \text{ ampère turns/metre}}$$

B. The air gap in a magnetic circuit is 1·0 mm long. The magnetising force required to set up a certain value of flux in this gap is found to be 200 000 ampère turns per metre. Calculate:

(a) the number of ampère turns required for the gap;
(b) the current required if the circuit is energised by a coil of 1000 turns.

(a) $$H = \frac{I \times N}{l}$$

$$200\,000 = \frac{I \times N}{1\cdot0/1000}$$

in this case l is the length of the air gap

$$\therefore I \times N = 200\,000 \times \frac{1\cdot0}{1000}$$

$$= \underline{200 \text{ ampère turns}}$$

(b) $$I \times N = 200$$

$$I \times 1000 = 200$$

$$\therefore I = \frac{200}{1000}$$

$$= \underline{0\cdot2A}$$

Permeability

In air, $\qquad B = H \times \mu_0$

and $\qquad \mu_0 = 4\pi \times 10^{-7},$

where μ_0 is the permeability of free space.

C. Calculate the flux density produced in air by a magnetising force of 20 000 At/m (ampère turns per metre).

$$B = H \times \mu_0$$
$$= 20\,000 \times 4\pi \times 10^{-7}$$
$$= \frac{20\,000 \times 4\pi}{10\,000\,000}$$
$$= \frac{25 \cdot 1 \times 10\,000}{10\,000\,000}$$
$$= 0 \cdot 025 \text{ Tesla (T) or Wb/m}^2$$

D. Determine the magnetising force required to produce a flux density of $1 \cdot 2$ mT in air.

$$B = H \times \mu_0$$
$$\frac{1 \cdot 2}{1000} = \frac{4\pi}{10^7} \times H$$

(note the conversion of mT to T)

$$\therefore \quad H = \frac{1 \cdot 2 \times 10\,000\,000}{4 \times \pi \times 1000}$$
$$= 955 \text{ At/m}$$

E. The air gap in a certain machine is $0 \cdot 5$ m^2 in cross-section and is 5 mm long. The magnetising force is provided by a coil of 1000 turns. Calculate the current which must flow in the coil to produce a total flux of $0 \cdot 25$ Wb in the gap.

Find the flux density.

$$\Phi = B \times A$$
$$0 \cdot 25 = B \times 0 \cdot 5$$
$$\therefore \quad B = \frac{0 \cdot 25}{0 \cdot 5}$$
$$= 0 \cdot 5 \text{T}$$

74

Find the magnetising force.

$$B = H \times \mu_0$$

$$0{\cdot}5 = H \times 4\pi \times 10^{-7}$$

$$\therefore H = \frac{0{\cdot}5}{4\pi \times 10^{-7}}$$

$$= \frac{0{\cdot}5 \times 10\,000\,000}{4\pi}$$

$$= 398\,000 \text{ At/m}$$

Ampère turns required for gap,

$$H = \frac{I \times N}{l}$$

$$398\,000 = \frac{I \times N}{5/1000}$$

$$\therefore I \times N = 398\,000 \times \frac{5}{1000}$$

$$= 1990$$

Find the current.

$$I \times N = 1990$$

$$I \times 1000 = 1990$$

$$\therefore I = \frac{1990}{1000}$$

$$= \underline{1{\cdot}99\text{A}}$$

Relative Permeability. In magnetic materials

$$B = H \times \mu_0 \times \mu_r$$

where μ_r is the relative permeability of the steel.

F. Calculate the flux density produced by a magnetising force of 2000 At/m in a steel of relative permeability 400.

$$B = H \times \mu_0 \times \mu_r$$

$$= \frac{2000 \times 4\pi \times 400}{10\,000\,000}$$

$$= \underline{1{\cdot}01\text{T}}$$

G. A mild steel ring 200 mm^2 in cross-sectional area and 0·2 m in mean diameter is wound with 450 turns of wire. Assuming that the steel has a relative permeability of 600, calculate the total flux produced in the ring when a current of 2A flows in the coil.

Find the magnetising force.

$$H = \frac{I \times N}{l}$$

(in this case l is the mean circumference of the ring)

$$= \frac{2 \times 450}{0·2 \times \pi}$$

$$= 1430 \text{ At/m}$$

Find the flux density produced.

$$B = H \times \mu_0 \times \mu_r$$

$$= \frac{1430 \times 4 \times \pi \times 600}{10\,000\,000}$$

$$= 1·08\text{T}$$

Find total flux.

$$\Phi = B \times A$$

$$= 1·08 \times \frac{200}{1\,000\,000}$$

$$= 0·000216 \text{ Wb}$$

$$= 0·216 \text{ mWb}$$

H. The relationship between the flux density and the magnetising force required in a certain brand of steel is

B (T)	0·8	1·0	1·2
H At/m	240	400	650

A ring is formed from this steel 50 mm^2 in cross-section and 0·1 m in mean diameter. A coil of 2500 turns is wound evenly upon it. Calculate the current which must flow in the coil to magnetise the steel to a flux density of 1·1T.

A graph to show the relationship between flux density and magnetising force can be plotted from the information given.

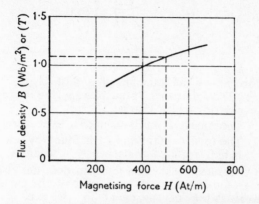

From the graph the magnetising force required to set up a flux density of 1·1T in this steel is 500 At/m.

$$H = \frac{I \times N}{l}$$

m.m.f. required

$$I \times N = H \times l$$
$$= 500 \times 0 \cdot 1\pi$$
$$= 50\pi \text{ At}$$
$$I = \frac{50\pi}{2500} \frac{\text{A}l}{l}$$
$$= \underline{0 \cdot 0628 \text{A}}$$

J. If a sawcut 1 mm wide is now made through the ring of example H as shown in the diagram, determine the current which now must flow in order to produce the same flux density as before.

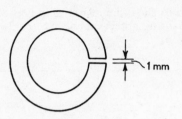

1 mm

This is now an example of a series type magnetic circuit. The same general principles apply to it as apply in series electric circuits. That is:

(1) The same *total* flux is assumed to exist at each point.
(2) The total m.m.f. required is found by adding the m.m.fs. required to magnetise the separate sections.

It is assumed that the 1 mm gap does not effectively change the length of the iron part of the circuit, this remains as 0.1π m. The m.m.f. for the steel portion is thus

$$50\pi = 157.1 \text{ At as before}$$

For the gap

$$\frac{B}{H} = \mu_0$$

$$\frac{1.1}{H} = 4\pi \times 10^{-7}$$

$$H = \frac{1.1}{4\pi \times 10^{-7}}$$

$$= \frac{1.1}{4\pi} \times 10^7$$

$$= 875\,200 \text{ At/m}$$

$$\text{m.m.f} = H \times l$$

$$\text{m.m.f} = 875\,200 \times \frac{1}{1000}$$

(here l is the length of the gap, and note the conversion to metres)

$$= 875.2 \text{ At}$$

78

The total m.m.f. required

$$= 157 \cdot 1 + 875 \cdot 2$$
$$= 1032 \cdot 3 \text{ At}$$

and the magnetising current

$$= \frac{1032 \cdot 3}{2500} \frac{\text{At}}{\text{t}}$$
$$= \underline{0 \cdot 413 \text{A}}$$

No allowance has been made for the effects of leakage and fringing but this magnetic circuit is typical of that found in many types of relay and transformer core.

K. A magnetic circuit has the form shown.

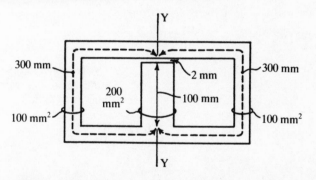

The material is the same as that used in examples H and J.

The centre limb is provided with a winding of 1000 turns. Determine the current required in this winding to produce a total flux in the air gap of 0·12 mWb.

It will be noticed that the magnetic circuit is symmetrical about the line YY that is, the outside limbs are identical in every respect. This is typical of many magnetic circuits such as are found in relay and transformer cores, d.c. machines, etc. If the effects of leakage and fringing are ignored, the circuit may be folded about the line YY so forming the equivalent series circuit thus:

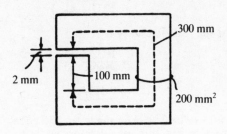

We now proceed as in examples H and J.

In the gap $\qquad \Phi = B \times A$

$$\frac{0\cdot12}{10^3} = \frac{B \times 200}{10^6}$$

(Note conversions of milliweber to weber and mm² to m²)

$$B = \frac{0\cdot12 \times 10^6}{200 \times 10^3}$$

$$= 0\cdot6 \text{T}$$

and $\qquad \dfrac{B}{H} = \mu_0$

$$\frac{0\cdot6}{H} = 4\pi \times 10^{-7}$$

$$H = \frac{0\cdot6}{4\pi \times 10^{-7}}$$

$$\text{m.m.f.} = H \times l$$

$$= \frac{0.6}{4\pi \times 10^{-7}} \times \frac{2}{1000}$$

$$= 954.8 \text{ At}$$

In the absence of leakage and fringing the flux density in the steel is the same as that in the air gap, that is 0·6T. By projecting the BH curve backwards slightly the necessary magnetising force is found to be approximately 130 At/m.

The total length of steel is 300 + 100 = 400 mm

the m.m.f. required for the steel is $130 \frac{\text{At}}{\cancel{\text{m}}} \times \frac{400}{1000} \cancel{\text{m}}$

$$= 52 \text{ At}$$

The total m.m.f. $\qquad = 52 + 954.8$

$$= 1006.8 \text{ At}$$

$$\text{say } 1000 \text{ At}$$

the magnetising current $\qquad = \dfrac{1000 \text{ A}\cancel{\text{t}}}{1000 \cancel{\text{t}}}$

$$= \underline{1\text{A}}$$

Exercises 8

1. Complete the following table:

Flux density B (T)	1·2	1·3			0·45
Cross-sectional area A (m²)	0·5	0·006	0·65	0·002	0·035
Total flux Φ (Wb)			520 mWb	1000 mWb	

2. The air gap of a contactor is 25 mm in diameter. Calculate the total flux when the flux density is 0·9T.

3. A magnetic circuit has a cross-sectional area of $0.75 \, \text{m}^2$ Calculate the flux density when the total flux is 0.6 Wb.

4. The air gap of a moving-coil instrument is 15 by 25 mm. Determine the flux density when the total flux in the gap is 0.3 mWb.

5. Calculate the magnetising force produced by a 350-turn coil carrying a current of 0.6A when it is attached to a magnetic circuit 0.5 m long.

6. An air gap is 2 mm long and the magnetising force required to set up a certain flux is 350 000 At/m. Find the number of ampère turns actually required for the gap.

7. The current available to set up a certain flux density in an air gap 5 mm long is 2A. The magnetising force required is found to be 200 000 At/m. Find the number of turns required on the coil.

8. A coil of 3500 turns is attached to a magnetic circuit 237 mm long. The magnetising force required to set up a certain flux is 8000 At/m. Calculate the current which must flow in the coil.

9. Calculate the flux density produced in air by the following values of magnetising force.
   (a) 20 000 At/m,
   (b) 105 000 At/m,
   (c) 750 000 At/m.

10. Complete the following table which refers to a certain air gap.

Flux density B (T)	1.2	0.012		0.5		0.95
Magnetising force H (At/m)			430000		3400	

11. Plot a graph showing the relationship between flux density and magnetising force for an air gap. Take values of H between 0 and 100 000 At/m.

12. The air gap in a certain magnetic circuit is 2.5 mm long and 350 mm² in cross-section. Calculate the magnetising force required to produce a total flux of 0.1 mWb in the gap.

13. A certain magnetic circuit is energised by a coil of 250 turns. An air gap in the circuit is 25 mm in diameter and 1 mm long. Calculate the current which must flow in the coil to produce a total flux of 750 μWb in the gap. (Neglect the m.m.f. required for the steel.)

14. A circular steel core is 20 mm by 20 mm in cross-section and 0·15m in mean diameter. It is provided with a coil of 500 turns. Using the figures given below calculate the current which must flow in the coil to produce a total flux of 0·5 mWb in the core.

Flux density B (T)	1·3	1·4	1·5
Magnetising force H (At/m)	800	1250	2000

15. If a radial air gap 1·5 mm wide is introduced into the core in question 14, calculate the current now required to produce the same total flux.

16. The magnetic circuit of a contactor is 0·3 m long and 15 mm by 25 mm in cross-section. The operating coil consists of 1500 turns of wire. Using the figures given below calculate the total flux produced in the core by a current of 0·067A.

Flux density B (T)	0·2	0·8	1·0
Magnetising force At/m	100	240	400

17. A steel ring of circular cross-section 150 mm² in area has a mean diameter of 85 mm. It is wound with 250 turns of wire. Assuming that the steel has relative permeability 500, calculate the current which must flow in the coil to produce a total flux in the steel of 0·035 mWb.

18. The ring of question 19 now has a radial air gap 0·5 mm wide inserted in it. Calculate the current which is required to produce the same flux as before.

19. A coil of insulated wire of 400 turns and of resistance 0·25 ohm, is wound tightly round an iron ring, and is connected to a d.c. supply of 4 volts. The iron ring is of uniform cross-sectional area 600 mm² and of mean diameter 0·15 m. The permeability of the ring may be taken as 450.
    Calculate the total flux in the iron.
    What would be the effect of an air gap in the ring? (C & G)

20. A coil of insulated wire of 500 turns and of resistance 4 ohms is closely wound on an iron ring. The ring has a uniform cross-sectional area of 700 mm² and a mean diameter of 0·25 m.
    Calculate the total flux in the ring when a d.c. supply at 6V is applied to the ends of the winding. Assume a relative permeability of 550.
    Explain the general effect of making a small air gap by cutting the ring radially at one point. (C & G)

21. The magnetic core of a contactor has the form shown. It is made from 12 stampings each 1 mm thick. Using the B-H values given in question 18, determine the total m.m.f. required to produce a flux density of 0·9T in the air gap.

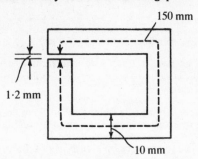

150 mm

1·2 mm

10 mm

22. A magnetic circuit has the form shown. A winding on the centre limb has 1500 turns. It is required to produce a total flux in the air gap of 0·25 mWb. The relative permeability of the steel under these conditions is 12 000. Determine the magnetising current.

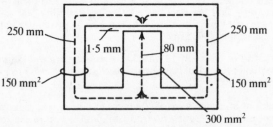

250 mm   250 mm

1·5 mm   80 mm

150 mm² — 150 mm²

300 mm²

23. Repeat question 22 using the magnetising curve of question 16.

ELECTROMAGNETISM II

References: **Growth and decay of current
in inductive circuits.
Energy stored in magnetic circuits.
Discharge resistors.**

Direct-current Excited Circuit having Inductance and Resistance in Series

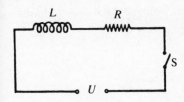

If such a circuit having inductance L henry in series with resistance R ohm is supplied at U volts d.c. the current at any instant t seconds after closing the switch S is found as follows:

(1) Calculate the final value of current $I = U/R$.
(2) Calculate the time constant $T = L/R$ (seconds).
(3) Draw graph axes to suitable scales. (The time required for the current to reach its maximum value may be taken as five times the time constant.)

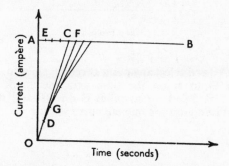

(4) Draw the horizontal line AB so that $OA = I$. Mark off $AC = T$. Join OC. Select any point D on OC. Project upwards vertically from D to E on AB, mark $EF = T$. Join FD. Repeat for the new point G on DF and so on until the complete curve is traced.

If immediately before the supply is disconnected the coil is connected to a resistor r, the current decays in a manner illustrated graphically as follows:

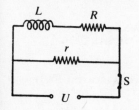

(a) Calculate the initial value of current $I = U/R$.

(b) Calculate the time constant

$$T = \frac{L}{R+r}$$

85

(5) Draw axes to suitable scale. Again the time required for the current to fall to zero may be taken as five times the time constant.

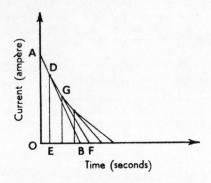

(6) Mark OA = I and OB = T.
Join AB and select any point D on AB close to A. Project from D to E on the time axis and mark EF = T. Join DF. Select a new point G on DF and repeat the procedure until a complete curve is formed.

Examples

A. A relay has a coil of resistance 480Ω and inductance 4·8H. It is connected to a 240-V d.c. supply. At the end of 0·05 second the coil is short circuited and the supply disconnected.

    (a) Draw curves showing the growth and decay of current plotted against time.

    (b) If the relay closes when the current reaches 0·3A increasing and opens when it reaches 0·15A decreasing, estimate the total time for which the relay contacts are closed.

Final value of current

$$I = \frac{U}{R}$$

$$= \frac{240}{480} = 0·5A$$

Time constant during increase of current

$$T = \frac{L}{R}$$

$$= \frac{4 \cdot 8}{480}$$

$$= 0 \cdot 01 \text{ second}$$

Since the coil is short circuited during the decay period the total circuit resistance is the same and the time constant remains unchanged.

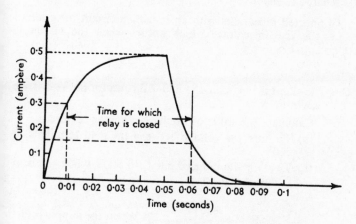

Total time for which relay is closed = $0 \cdot 05 - 0 \cdot 0092$

$$+ 0 \cdot 012$$

$$= 0 \cdot 0528 \text{ second}$$

$$= \underline{52 \cdot 8 \text{ millisecond}}$$

Energy Stored

The energy stored in a circuit of inductance L henry when the current flowing is I ampère is

$$W = \tfrac{1}{2}LI^2 \text{ Joule}$$

B. Calculate the maximum energy stored in the relay of the previous example.

The maximum current $I = \dfrac{U}{R}$

$$= \dfrac{240}{480} = 0.5\text{A}$$

$$W = \tfrac{1}{2}LI^2$$
$$= \tfrac{1}{2} \times 4.8 \times (0.5)^2$$
$$= \underline{0.6\text{J}}$$

Discharge Resistor

Connected in parallel with an inductive circuit in order to limit the rise in voltage which occurs when the circuit is interrupted.

C. The shunt field circuit of a 250-V d.c. motor has resistance 125Ω.

Calculate the value of discharge resistor required:
(a) To limit the voltage between the field terminals to 500V.
(b) To limit the induced e.m.f. to 500V when the field circuit is broken.

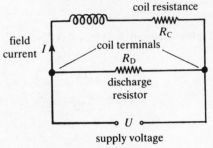

coil resistance
R_C
field current I coil terminals
R_D
discharge resistor
U
supply voltage

When the supply is disconnected the current decays in the loop formed by R_C and R_D. At this instant the current in this loop is

$$I = \dfrac{U}{R_C}$$

in this case $I = \dfrac{250}{125}$

$$= \underline{2\text{A}}$$

88

(a) The voltage between the coil terminals is the voltage across the discharge resistor which is $I \times R_D$

i.e.
$$500 = I \times R_D$$
$$R_D = \frac{500}{2}$$
$$= \underline{250\Omega}$$

(b) By applying Kirchhoff's law to the closed loop referred to above

induced e.m.f.
$$E = IR_C + IR_D$$
$$500 = 2 \times 125 + 2 \times R_D$$
$$2 \times R_D = 500 - 250$$
$$R_D = \frac{250}{2}$$
$$= \underline{125\Omega}$$

Exercises 9

1. A coil has inductance 1·5H and resistance 50Ω. Construct a curve showing the variation in current with time when this coil is connected to a 10-V d.c. supply.

2. A coil having inductance 0·25H and resistance 250Ω is connected in parallel with a resistance of 250Ω to a d.c. supply of 50V. Construct a curve showing the variation in current with time from the instant that the d.c. supply is disconnected.

3. The following figures show the variation in current with time when a coil of resistance 10Ω and unknown inductance is connected to a d.c. supply of 100V.

Current (A)	0	3·297	5·501	7·534	8·347	8·892	9·502
time (s)	0	0·4	0·8	1·4	1·8	2·2	3·0

Given that the time constant L/R is equal to the time required for the current to rise to 0·632 of its maximum value, calculate the inductance of the coil.

4. A relay coil has resistance 1250Ω and inductance 0·25H. A d.c. voltage pulse which rises instantly to 50V remains constant for 0·0015 second and then falls instantly to zero is applied to the coil. The voltage source may be assumed to have negligible resistance. Construct a curve showing the variation in current through the coil. If the relay closes when the current reaches 30 mA increasing and opens when the current falls to 15 mA decreasing, determine the total time for which the relay contacts are closed.

5. Calculate the maximum energy stored in each of the magnetic circuits of examples 13 to 16 inclusive in exercises 8.*

6. The field system of a d.c. motor has four coils in series. Each coil has 1000 turns and resistance 20Ω. When the supply voltage is 240V the flux per pole is 0·05 Wb, when the voltage is 120V the flux per pole is 0·03 Wb. Calculate the energy stored in the field system under normal running conditions when the voltage is 240V.*

7. The field system of a 400-V d.c. motor has total resistance 100Ω. Calculate the value of a discharge resistor which will limit the induced e.m.f. to 1000V when the field circuit is broken.

8. A 500-V d.c. generator has six poles connected in series Each pole has 750 turns and resistance 15Ω. A change in current of 2·5A through the winding produces a change in flux of 0·06 Wb. Calculate:

   (a) the inductance of the field system;*
   (b) the energy stored during normal working;
   (c) the value of a discharge resistor necessary to limit the e.m.f. induced when the circuit is broken to 1000V.
   (d) the energy dissipated in the discharge resistor.

D.C. GENERATOR CALCULATIONS

References: **Generator e.m.f. equation.**
Terminal voltage/load current
Characteristics.

The e.m.f. generated by a d.c. generator is

* *hint*: use the definition $\text{Inductance} = \dfrac{\text{change in flux linkages}}{\text{change in magnetising current}}$

$$E = \frac{\Phi \times Z \times n \times p}{c}$$

E is the e.m.f. in volts

Φ is the useful flux per pole in weber

Z is the number of armature conductors

p is the number of poles

c is the number of armature circuits

$c = p$ for a lap winding

$c = 2$ for a wave winding

n is the speed in rev/s

The terminal voltage is given by

$$U = E - I_a R_a$$

U is the terminal voltage in volts

E is the generated e.m.f. in volts

I_a is the armature current in ampères

R_a is armature resistance in ohms

Examples

A. Calculate the terminal voltage of a d.c. generator to which the following particulars refer, when it carries a load of 25A.

Field: 4 poles separately excited, useful flux per pole 0·025 Wb.

Armature: 800 conductors, lap connected, total resistance 0·Ω, speed of rotation 15 rev/s

$$E = \frac{\Phi \times Z \times n \times p}{c}$$

$$= \frac{0{\cdot}025 \times 800 \times 15 \times 4}{4}$$

$$= 300V$$

$$U = E - I_a R_a$$
$$= 300 - 25 \times 0{\cdot}1$$
$$= 300 - 2{\cdot}5$$
$$= \underline{297{\cdot}5V}$$

B. A d.c. generator delivers a load current of 50A at a terminal voltage of 200V. The total resistance of its armature circuit is 0·15Ω and there is a 2-volt drop at the brushes. Calculate:

(a) the generated e.m.f.;

(b) the speed at which it must be driven given the following information:

Number of poles 6, separately excited.

Useful flux per pole 0·04 Wb.

Number of armature conductors 600, lap connection.

(a)
$$U = E - I_a R_a$$
$$200 = E - 50 \times 0·15 - 2$$
$$E = 200 + 2 + 7·5$$
$$= \underline{209·5\text{V}}$$

(b)
$$E = \frac{\Phi \times n \times Z \times p}{c}$$
$$209·5 = \frac{0·04 \times n \times 600 \times 6}{6}$$
$$= 24n$$
$$n = \frac{209·5}{24}$$
$$= \underline{8·73 \text{ rev/s}}$$

Many syllabuses do not require the full use of the e.m.f. equation, so the following examples are based upon typical examination questions.

C. A load of 20.2 kW at 230 V is supplied by a shunt wound d.c. generator.

The shunt field has a resistance of 110 Ω and the armature a resistance (including brushes) of 0.25 Ω. Brush contact volts drop is 1·9 V.

Calculate the:

(i) armature current

(ii) generated e.m.f.
(iii) total electrical losses.

(i) Load current $(I) = \dfrac{P}{U} = \dfrac{20 \cdot 2 \times 1000}{230}$

$= 87 \cdot 83$ A

Field current (If) $= \dfrac{U}{Rf} = \dfrac{230}{110}$

Armature current (Ia) $= I + If = 87 \cdot 83 + 2 \cdot 09$
$\quad = \underline{89 \cdot 92 \text{ A}}$

(ii) Terminal voltage = generated e.m.f. – armature volts drop – brush contact volts drop.
Thus $U = E - I_a R_a - 1 \cdot 9$
and $E = U + I_a R_a + 1 \cdot 9$
$\quad = 230 + (89 \cdot 92 \times 0 \cdot 25) + 1 \cdot 9$
$\quad = 230 + 22 \cdot 48 + 1 \cdot 9$
$\quad = \underline{254 \cdot 38 \text{ V}}$

(iii) Copper losses in armature winding $I_a{}^2 R_a = 89 \cdot 92^2 \times 0 \cdot 25$
$\qquad\qquad\qquad\qquad\qquad\qquad\qquad = 2021 \cdot 4$ W
Copper losses in field winding $(If^2 Rf) \quad = 2 \cdot 09^2 \times 110$
$\qquad\qquad\qquad\qquad\qquad\qquad\qquad = 480 \cdot 49$ W
Total electrical losses $\qquad\qquad\qquad = \quad 2021 \cdot 4 \quad +$
$480 \cdot 49$
$= 2501 \cdot 89$ W

D. A 200 V d.c. generator runs at 25 rev/s and supplies a load current of 15 A. If the input torque to the generator shaft is 26 Nm, determine the generator:
  (i) efficiency at this load
  (ii) power loss at this load

(i) efficiency $= \dfrac{UI}{T(2\pi n)} \times 100$

$= \dfrac{200 \times 15 \times 100}{26 \times 2\pi \times 25}$

$$= 73.46 \%$$

(ii) input power = output power + losses
thus $T, (2\pi n) = UI$ + losses
so losses $= T (2\pi n) - UI$
$$= (26 \times 2\pi \times 25) \ (200 \times 15)$$
$$= 4084 - 3000$$
$$= 1084 \text{ W}$$

Exercise 10

1. Explain the function of a commutator in a direct-current generator.

   A load of 19·2 kW is supplied from the terminals of a 2-pole d.c. shunt generator at 240V. The shunt winding of the generator has a resistance of 96Ω, and the resistance of the armature is 0·2Ω. There is a brush-contact volts drop of 2V.

   Calculate:

   (*a*) the current in the armature,

   (*b*) the e.m.f. generated, and

   (*c*) the copper losses in the machine.   (C & G)

2. A d.c. generator supplies a load of 80A through cables which have total resistance 0·05Ω. Its armature circuit resistance is 0·1Ω and there is a 1-V drop at the brushes. Calculate its generated e.m.f. in order that the voltage at the load end shall be 200V.

3. A d.c. generator to which the following particulars refer delivers 40A at a terminal voltage of 500V. Calculate the useful flux per pole.

   Number of poles: 4.

   Armature winding: 700 conductors, wave connected total resistance 0·1Ω.

   Speed of rotation 10 rev/s.

4. Calculate the speed at which a d.c. generator must be driven in order to deliver 30A at a terminal voltage of 450V given the following details:

   Number of poles 4;

   Number of armature conductors 600;

   Useful flux per pole 0·03 Wb;

   Type of winding wave;

   Resistance of armature 0·15Ω.

5. The following particulars refer to a certain shunt-connected d.c. generator:

   Number of poles 6;

   Armature winding 750 conductors lap-connected, total resistance 0·5Ω;

   Useful flux per pole 0·03 Wb;

   Resistance of field winding 150Ω;

   Brush-contact voltage drop 2V.

   Calculate the speed at which the machine must be driven in order to generate 12·5 kW at a terminal voltage of 250V.

6. The open circuit voltage of a d.c. generator is 250V. Calculate its open circuit voltage when the speed is increased by 20% and the flux is reduced by 15%.

7. A d.c. generator delivers 20A at 250V. Its efficiency is 72%. Calculate (i) the power required to drive it, (ii) the torque required in Nm if its speed if 16 rev/s.

8. A d.c. shunt generator has a shunt field resistance of 120 Ω and an armature resistance of 0·1 Ω. When supplying a load of 28 A at a terminal voltage of 240 V. Calculate the:
   (i) shunt field circuit current;
   (ii) armature current;
   (iii) e.m.f. generated.

9. A 200 V d.c. generator running at 25 rev/s supplies a current of 15 A. If the input torque to the generator shaft is 26 Nm, determine the:
   (i) efficiency of the generator
   (ii) generator power loss

10. A shunt-wound d.c. generator supplies a load of 18·4 kW at 230 V through a 2 core-cable of total resistance 0·05 Ω. The resistance of the armature is 0·03 Ω and there is a total brush contact drop of 2 V. The resistance of the field winding is 78 Ω. Calculate the generator terminal voltage and the generated e.m.f. (C & G)

11. A 240 V generator supplies a load of 25 kW. The shunt field resistance is 160 Ω and the armature resistance is 0·12 Ω. Assuming a brush contact voltage drop of 2 V, find the:
   (i) armature current
   (ii) generated e.m.f.
   (iii) copper losses in the windings. (C & G)

12. Tests being conducted on a diesel engine driven shunt wound d.c. generator produce the following results;
    (i)   input torque to generator   = 23 Nm
    (ii) output voltage   = 150 V
    (iii) armature current   = 14 A

The generator shunt field regulator is now set to reduce the flux to 80% and the input torque now increases to 33 Nm. What will the armature current be at this new torque.

13. A shunt-wound d.c. generator supplies a load of 18 kW at 240 V through a 2 core-cable of total resistance 0·055 Ω. The resistance of the armature is 0·033 Ω and there is a total voltage drop 2·4 V in the brush gear. The resistance of the shunt field is 79 Ω. Calculate the:
    (i)   load current
    (ii) voltage required at the generator terminals
    (iii) generator field current
    (iv) generator armature current
    (v) generated e.m.f.

D.C. MOTOR CALCULATIONS

References: **Direct-current motor, total torque
and shaft torque.
Factors influencing speed.
Efficiency.
Starting resistance.**

The total torque of a d.c. motor is given by

$$T = \Phi \times I_a \times \frac{Zp}{2\pi c} \quad \text{Nm}$$

where Φ is the useful flux per pole (Wb)
                I_a is the armature current (A)
                Z is the number of armature conductors
                p is the number of poles
                c is the number of armature circuits
                     ($c = p$ for lap windings
                     $c = 2$ for wave windings).

Examples

A. A d.c. motor develops total torque 150 Nm when its armature current is 25A and the useful flux per pole is 0·25 Wb. Calculate the total torque when the armature current increases to 35A and the flux is reduced to 0·2 Wb.

We may replace $Zp/2\pi c$ by k, a constant, in the torque equation.

Then
$$T = k \times \Phi \times I_a$$

If T_1 be the torque corresponding to flux Φ_1 and current I_1 and T_2 be the torque corresponding to flux Φ_2 and current I_2

$$T_1 = k \times \Phi_1 \times I_1 \qquad \text{(i)}$$

and
$$T_2 = k \times \Phi_2 \times I_2 \qquad \text{(ii)}$$

Dividing (ii) by (i)

$$\frac{T_2}{T_1} = \frac{\Phi_2 \times I_2}{\Phi_1 \times I_1} \quad k \text{ cancelling}$$

Calling T_2 the new value of torque

$$\frac{T_2}{150} = \frac{0·2 \times 35}{0·25 \times 25}$$

$$T_2 = \frac{150 \times 0·2 \times 35}{0·25 \times 25}$$

$$= \underline{168 \text{ Nm}}$$

B. Details of a d.c. motor are as follows:

Number of poles 6
Number of armature conductors 700
Useful flux per pole 0·056 Wb
Type of armature winding lap

Its armature current is 12A when it delivers 4·103 kW to a machine at 11 rev/s. Calculate the total torque and the shaft torque. Express these in the same units.

Total torque is calculated from the formula

$$T = \Phi \times I_a \times \frac{Zp}{2\pi c}$$

$$= 0 \cdot 056 \times 12 \times \frac{700 \times 6}{2\pi \times 6}$$

$$= \underline{74 \cdot 85 \text{ Nm}}$$

Shaft torque is calculated from the formula

$$P = 2\pi n T$$

> where P is in watts
> n is the speed in rev/s
> T is the torque in Nm

$$4103 = 2\pi \times 11 \times T$$

$$T = \frac{4103}{\pi \times 11}$$

$$= \underline{59 \cdot 36 \text{ Nm}}$$

Back e.m.f. and Speed

When the motor runs on load its speed is such that the equation $U = E + I_a R_a$ is satisfied.

U is the armature supply voltage
E is the back e.m.f.
I_a is the armature current
R_a is the resistance of the armature circuit

and E is given by the generator e.m.f. formula

$$E = \Phi \times n \times Z \times p$$

which is simplified to

$$E = k \times \Phi \times n \quad \text{where } k \text{ is a constant.}$$

Many syllabuses do not require the full use of the torque equation, so the following examples are based upon typical examination questions.

C. A 2.5 kW 250 V d.c. shunt-wound motor runs at 16 rev/s and takes a current of 14 A when developing full-load output. The armature resistance is 0·4 Ω and the field resistance is 160 Ω
Calculate at full load the:
   (i) armature current;
  (ii) back e.m.f;
 (iii) efficiency;
  (iv) shaft torque.

   (i) Armature current (Ia) = supply current – field current (If)
       Now $I_f = \dfrac{U}{Rf}$ where Rf is the resistance of shunt field
       $I_f = \dfrac{250}{160} = 1\cdot56\,A$
       And $I_a = 14\cdot0 - 1\cdot56 = 12\cdot44\,A$

  (ii) Back e.m.f. $Eb = U - I_aR_a$, where R_a is the resistance of armature
       Then $Eb = 250 - (12\cdot44 \times 0\cdot4)$
       $= 250 - 4\cdot98 = 245\cdot02\,V.$

 (iii) Efficiency $= \dfrac{\text{output}}{\text{input}} = \dfrac{2500}{250 \times 14}$

       $= \dfrac{2500 \times 100}{3500}$

       $= 71\cdot4\,\%$

  (iv) Shaft torque
       $\doteqdot \dfrac{2500}{2\pi \times 16};$
       $= 24\cdot87\,Nm$

99

D. A 20 kW, 240 V d.c. shunt motor has a full load efficiency of 80 %. The shunt field resistance is 106 Ω and the armature resistance (including brushes) is 0·12 Ω. Assuming a brush contact voltage drop of 2 V, determine at full load the:

   (i) armature current
   (ii) generated back e.m.f.
   (iii) total copper losses. (C & G)

$$
\begin{aligned}
\text{(i) Input to motor} &= \frac{20 \times 100}{80} \\
&= 25 \text{ kW} \\
\text{Full load current} &= \frac{25000}{240} \\
&= 104 \cdot 17 \text{ A} \\
\text{Field current } (I_f) &= \frac{240}{160} \\
&= 1 \cdot 5 \text{ A} \\
\text{Armature current } (I_a) &= 104 \cdot 17 - 1 \cdot 5 \\
&= \underline{102 \cdot 67 \text{ A}}
\end{aligned}
$$

$$
\begin{aligned}
\text{(ii) Back e.m.f.} \quad E_b &= U - I_a R_a - \text{brush volts drop} \\
&= 240 - (102 \cdot 67 \times 0 \cdot 12) - 2 \\
&= 240 - 12 \cdot 32 - 2 \\
&= \underline{225 \cdot 68 \text{ V}}
\end{aligned}
$$

$$
\begin{aligned}
\text{(iii) Total copper losses} &= \text{Cu loss in field} + \text{Cu loss in armature} \\
&= I_f^2 R_f + I_a^2 R_a \\
&= (1 \cdot 5^2 \times 160) + (102 \cdot 67^2 \times 0 \cdot 12) \\
&= 360 + 1265 \\
&= \underline{1 \cdot 625 \text{ kW}}
\end{aligned}
$$

E. A d.c. shunt motor-generator set running at 12 rev/s supplies a current of 13 A to an external load connected to the generator terminals. At this load the motor, connected to a 90 V supply, takes a current of 12 A.

Details of the machines at this load are as follows:

	Motor	Generator
armature resistance	$0 \cdot 4 \, \Omega$	$0 \cdot 2 \, \Omega$
field current	2 A	1 A
constant losses	114 W	46 W

Calculate the:

(i) mechanical power delivered to the motor shaft
(ii) motor output torque
(iii) efficiency of the motor-generator set. (C & G)

(i) Motor.
    Field copper losses $(I^2 R_f)$ $= 90 \times 2$ $= 180 \, W$
    Armature current $= 12 - 2$ $= 10 \, A$
    Armature copper losses
        $(I^2 R_a) = 10^2 \times 0 \cdot 4 = 40 \, W$
    Electrical input (W) $= 90 \times 12$ $= 1080 \, W$
$\therefore$ Output power from motor $= 1080 - (114 + 180 + 40)$
        $= \underline{746 \, W}$

(ii) Motor output torque $= \dfrac{746}{2 \, \Omega \times 12} = \underline{9 \cdot 9 \, Nm}$

(iii) Generator.
    Mechanical input to
      generator $= 746 \, W$
    Armature current $= 13 + 1$ $= 14 \, A$
    Armature copper losses
      $(I^2 R_a)$ $= 14^2 \times 0 \cdot 2 = 39 \cdot 2 \, W$
    Armature output $= 746 - (46 + 39 \cdot 2)$
        $= 660 \cdot 8 \, W$

Generator output voltage $= \dfrac{660 \cdot 8}{14}$ $= 47 \cdot 2 \, V$

Generator output power $= 13 \times 47 \cdot 2 = 613 \cdot 6 \, W$
$\therefore$ Efficiency of motor-generator $= \dfrac{613 \cdot 6}{1080} \times 100 = \underline{56 \cdot 8\%}$

F. On no-load the speed of a d.c. motor is 16 rev/s. Calculate the speed when the load is such that the armature current is 25A. The terminal voltage is constant at 400V, the armature resistance is 0·15Ω and armature reaction is to be neglected.

If the no-load armature current is neglected the equation

$$U = E + I_a R_a \quad \text{reduces to}$$

$$U = E \qquad \text{i.e. the back e.m.f. is equal to the supply voltage.}$$

Also if armature reaction is neglected the flux is constant

and $$E = kn$$

as shown previously, if $E_1, n_1 : E_2, n_2$ are corresponding values

$$\frac{E_2}{E_1} = \frac{n_2}{n_1}$$

Thus if $n_1 = 16$ and n_2 is to be calculated, first calculate E_2

$$U = E_2 + I_a R_a$$

$$400 = E_2 + 25 \times 0\cdot15$$

$$E = 400 - 3\cdot75$$

$$= 396\cdot25\text{V}$$

Then $$\frac{n_2}{16} = \frac{396\cdot25}{400} \quad (E_1 = U = 400)$$

$$n_2 = 16 \times \frac{396\cdot25}{400}$$

$$= \underline{15\cdot85 \text{ rev/s}}$$

Efficiency Tests

Direct Method

G. A test on a d.c. motor yielded the following results:

Electrical input
    Terminal voltage 460V
    Supply current 18·9A

Mechanical output from brake test
    Diameter of brake pulley 0·4 m
    Nett brake load 320N
    Speed 16 rev/s

Calculate the efficiency at this condition

Torque $\qquad T = F \times r$

where F is the nett brake load (N)

r is the pulley radius (m)

$$T = 320 \times \frac{0·4}{2}$$

$$= 62 \text{ Nm}$$

Mechanical output $= 2\pi nT$ W

$$= 2\pi \times 16 \times 62$$

$$= 6233 \text{ W}$$

Electrical input $= 460 \times 18·9$

$$= 8694 \text{W}$$

Efficiency $= \dfrac{\text{output}}{\text{input}}$

$$= \frac{6233}{8694}$$

$$= 0·7169$$

or $\underline{71·69\%}$

Indirect Method

H. A no-load test on a d.c. shunt motor produced the following results:

> Supply voltage   400V
> Armature current   3·5A   Speed 12·5 rev/s
> Armature resistance   0·8Ω
> Field resistance   120Ω

Predict the efficiency and speed of the machine when the load is such that the armature current is 40A.

This is the 'summation of losses' method of determining efficiency. The various losses to be calculated are:

(a) Field circuit copper loss   } assumed
(b) Iron friction and windage loss } constant
(c) Armature copper loss varying with the square of the load.

for (a) Field copper loss $= \dfrac{U^2}{R_f}$

$$= \frac{400^2}{120}$$

$$= 1333\text{W}$$

(b) This is the total input to the armature on no load

$$= 400 \times 3\cdot5$$

$$= 1400\text{W}$$

Total constant loss $= 1333 + 1400$

$$= 2733\text{W}$$

for (c) corresponding to an armature current of 40A the armature copper loss

$$= I_a^2 R_a$$

$$= 40^2 \times 0\cdot8$$

$$= 1280\text{W}$$

Total losses $= 2733 + 1280$

$$= 4013\text{W}$$

Efficiency $\qquad = \dfrac{\text{input}}{\text{input} + \text{losses}}$

$$= \frac{400 \times 40}{(400 \times 40) + 4013}$$

$$= 0.795 \text{ or } \underline{79.5\%}$$

The speed is calculated as in example D.

Thus on no load $\qquad U = E_1$ (approximately)

or $\qquad\qquad\qquad E_1 = 400$

and on load of 40A, $\quad 400 = E_2 + 40 \times 0.8$

$$E_2 = 400 - 32$$

$$= 368\text{V}$$

and $\qquad\qquad\qquad \dfrac{n_2}{n_1} = \dfrac{E_2}{E_1}$

> where n_2 is the required speed and n_1 is the no-load speed

$$n_2 = 12.5 \times \frac{368}{400}$$

$$= \underline{11.5 \text{ rev/s}}$$

(What assumptions have been made in this example?)

Starting Resistance

I. The armature of a 400-V, 30-kW motor has resistance 0.65Ω. Assuming that the full-load efficiency of the motor is 75%, calculate the value of the series resistor which will limit the starting current to $1\frac{1}{2}$ times its full-load value.

The full-load current is calculated as follows:

full-load output (watts) $= 30 \times 1000$

full-load input $\qquad\quad = 30 \times 1000 \times \dfrac{100}{75}\text{W}$

$$\text{full-load current} = \frac{30 \times 1000 \times 100}{400 \times 75}$$

$$= 100\text{A}$$

$$1\tfrac{1}{2} \times \text{full-load current} = \tfrac{3}{2} \times 100$$

$$= 150\text{A}$$

In the absence of back e.m.f.

$$U = I_a R_a$$

where R_a is the total armature circuit resistance

$$400 = 150 \times R_a$$

$$R_a = \frac{400}{150}$$

$$= 2{\cdot}667\Omega$$

Value of the additional series resistance is thus

$$2{\cdot}667 - 0{\cdot}65 = 2{\cdot}017\Omega$$

$$\text{or } \underline{2{\cdot}02\Omega}$$

Exercise 11

1. A d.c. motor develops a torque of 200 Nm under given conditions of flux and armature current. Calculate the torque when the armature current falls by 12% and the flux increases by 8%.

2. A d.c. shunt motor connected to a 240 V supply, has a no-load speed of 24·6 rev/s. The current input at no-load is 5 A, and at full load 42 A. The armature resistance is 0·2 Ω, and the shunt winding resistance is 160 Ω.
   Calculate the speed of the motor at full load (C & G)

3. The armature resistance of a d.c. motor is 0·1 Ω. On no-load it runs at a speed of 20 rev/s from a 250 V supply. Calculate the speed at which it will run when its armature current is 15 A. The supply voltage and magnetic flux remain constant.

4. Calculate the total torque developed by a d.c. motor to which the following details refer:
   Number of poles 4
   Number of armature conductors 740
   Useful flux per pole 0·3 Wb
   Type of winding, wave
   armature current 20 A.

5. Calculate the value of armature current required in the motor of question 4 in order for it to develop a total torque of 1200 Nm, all other conditions remaining constant.

6. A d.c. motor runs at 13 rev/s when its armature current is 25 A and the terminal voltage is 250 V. Its armature resistance is 0·12 Ω. Calculate the speed at which it must be driven as a generator in order for it to deliver 25 A at a terminal voltage of 250 V, the flux remaining constant.

7. A 460 V, d.c. shunt running on no-load at 46·6 rev/s, takes a current of 6A. The resistance of the field winding is 230 Ω and the resistance of the armature circuit is 0·3 Ω.
   Calculate the speed of the motor when it runs with a full load input of 35 A. Assume that the field current remains constant.

8. A 250 V d.c. shunt motor runs at 11 rev/s when the input current is 42 A. The armature circuit resistance is 0·25 Ω, the shunt field resistance is 62·5 Ω and the sum of the iron, friction and windage losses is 1400 W.
   Calculate the:
     (i) motor output
     (ii) motor efficiency
     (iii) shaft torque   (C & G)

9. A 2·5 kW, 220 V d.c. shunt-wound motor runs at 18 rev/s and takes a current of 18 A when developing full-load output. The armature resistance is 0 .3 Ω and the field resistance is 180 Ω.
   Calculate at full load the:
     (i)   armature current
     (ii) back e.m.f
     (iii) efficiency
     (iv) torque

10. The resistance of armature and shunt field respectively of a d.c. motor are 0·15 Ω and 250 Ω. On no-load when the armature current may be neglected, the speed is 10 rev/s. Calculate the speed when the load is such that the total input current is 35 A. Assume constant terminal voltage of 400 V.

11. A d.c. shunt motor connected to a 240 V d.c. supply has a no-load speed of 24·5 rev/s. The current input at no-load is 4 A, and full-load the current input is 38 A. The shunt field-windings have a resistance of 150 Ω and the resistance of the armature is 0 .25 Ω.
    Calculate the speed at full load.

12. The following readings were taken during a brake test on a d.c. motor.
    Brake load   196 N at an effective radius of 460 mm
    Speed   20 rev/s
    Electrical input   57 A at 250 V
    Calculate the efficiency of the motor at this load.

13. The following readings were taken during a brake test on a A d.c. motor.
    Speed of motor   24 rev/s
    Effective diameter of brake pulley   250 mm
    Effective pull at circumference of pulley   220 N
    Electrical input   5800 W
    Find the power output and the efficiency at this load (C & G)

14. A d.c. motor runs at 12·5 rev/s on no-load when its terminal voltage is 250 V. The input is 800 W. The armature resistance is 0·6 Ω. Calculate the efficiency under the same conditions of terminal voltage and speed when the armature current is (i) 30 A, (ii) 50 A.

15. The armature of a d.c. motor has a resistance of 0·45 Ω and takes a full-load current of 50 A from a 400 V supply. Calculate the value of additional series resistance required to limit the starting current to 1½ times the full-load value.

16. A 200 V, 7·5 kW d.c. motor operates with a full-load efficiency of 70%. Its armature resistance is 0·8 Ω. Calculate the value of series resistance required to limit the starting current to 1½ times the full-load value.

17. Calculate the ohmic value of a starting resistor for the following d.c. shunt motor:

Output — 14 920 W
Supply — 240 V
Armature resistance — 0·25 Ω
Efficiency at full-load — 86%

The starting current is to be limited to 1½ times full-load current. Ignore the current in the shunt winding.

18. A 460 V d.c. motor runs at 15·8 rev/s and develops 7460 W with an efficiency of 85%. The armature resistance is 0·2 Ω. Calculate the value of resistor which when connected in series with the armature will reduce the speed to 11·7 rev/s, the armature current remaining constant.

UTILISATION OF ELECTRIC POWER I

References: **Torque, work and power. Power in
Efficiency of machines. d.c. and a.c. circuits.**

Examples

A. A load of 100 kg is raised through a vertical distance of 12 m in 15 s by a hoist. The efficiency of the hoist gearing is 30% and that of the driving motor is 80%. Calculate the electrical power input to the motor.

The force required to lift a load of 1 kg against the effect of gravity is 9·81 N.

(This is the same as saying that 1 kgf is equivalent to 9·81 N.)

Work done = distance × force

$$W = 12 \text{ m} \times 100 \times 9·81 \text{ N}$$

$$= 11\ 772 \text{ mN}$$

and 1 mN (or 1 Nm) = 1 J (Joule)

Thus the work done on the load

$$= 11\ 772\ \text{J}$$

and the work done per second

$$= \frac{11\ 772}{15}\ \text{J/s}$$

$$= 784 \cdot 8\text{W} \quad (\text{for } 1\ \text{J/s} = 1\text{W})$$

The input to the hoist gear which is the driving motor output

$$= 784 \cdot 8 \times \frac{100}{30}$$

$$= 2616\text{W}$$

The input to the driving motor

$$= 2616 \times \frac{100}{80}$$

$$= 3270\text{W}$$

$$\text{or } \underline{3 \cdot 27\ \text{kW}}$$

B. A pump raises $0 \cdot 0075\ \text{m}^3$ of water per second through a vertical height of 30 m. Its efficiency is 70% and it is driven by a 415-V 3-phase motor of efficiency 85% and power factor 0·8. Calculate the line current to the motor.

1 m³ of water weighs 1000 kgf

following the previous example—

Work done by the pump per second

$$= \frac{30 \times 0 \cdot 0075 \times 1000 \times 9 \cdot 81}{1}$$

$$= 2207\ \frac{\text{Nm}}{\text{s}} \quad \text{or} \quad \frac{\text{J}}{\text{s}} \quad \text{or} \quad \text{W}$$

electrical input to driving motor

$$= 2207 \times \frac{100}{70} \times \frac{100}{85}$$

$$= 3709\text{W}$$

The power in a 3-phase circuit

$$P = \sqrt{3}\, U_L I_L \cos \phi$$

$$3709 = \sqrt{3} \times 415 \times I_L \times 0.8$$

$$I_L = \frac{3709}{\sqrt{3} \times 415 \times 0.8}$$

$$= \underline{6.45\text{A}}$$

C. The cutting tool of a lathe experiences a force of 400 N when a work piece 150 mm in diameter is rotated against it at a speed of 2·66 rev/s. Calculate the power absorbed by the cutting operation.

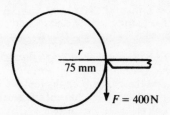

Torque = Force × radius of work piece

$$= 400 \times \frac{150}{2 \times 1000}$$

$$= 30\ \text{Nm}$$

$$P = 2\pi n T\ \text{W} \qquad \text{where } T \text{ is the torque in Nm and } n \text{ the speed in rev/min}$$

$$P = 2\pi \times 2.66 \times 30$$

$$= \underline{501.4\ \text{W}}$$

Exercises 12

1. A conveyor raises 250 kg of goods per minute through a vertical distance of 25 m. It is driven through a gearbox of efficiency 62%. Determine the power output of the driving motor.

2. A pump rotating at 16 rev/s raises 0·015 m³ of water per second through a vertical distance of 50 m. Calculate the torque required to drive it.

3. Calculate the torque required if the pump of question 2 is used to pump oil of relative density 0·78 under the same conditions.

4. A generator of efficiency 82% delivers 75A at 120V. Calculate the torque required to turn it at 16 rev/s.

5. A crane raises a load of 2000 kg at a speed of 0·45 m/s. The efficiency of the gearing is 55% and it is driven by a 250-V d.c. motor of efficiency 72%. Calculate the armature current.

6. The chuck of a lathe is driven at 2 rev/s through gearing which is 60% efficient. During a turning operation on a work-piece 75 mm in radius the pressure on the tool is 650 N. The driving motor is a 3-phase 415-V machine of efficiency 85% and power factor 0·75. Calculate the line current.

7. A brake test on a 3-phase motor yielded the following results:

line current 12A	speed 16 rev/s
line voltage 415V	brake tension tight side 227 N;
wattmeter readings 4986W,	slack side 40 N
982W	brake pulley diameter 0·5 m.

   Calculate the efficiency and the power factor at this load.

8. The cage of a lift weighs 1000 kg and can carry a maximum load of 1500 kg. The hoisting ropes pass over a driving sheave 1 m in diameter and are attached to a balance weight equal to the weight of the cage plus 40% of the maximum load. Assuming that the cage is three-quarters loaded and travelling upwards at a speed of 0·66 m/s. Calculate:

   (a) the speed at which the driving sheave rotates;
   (b) the torque required to turn it.

9. If the sheave of question 7 is driven by a 460-V d.c. motor of efficiency 70% through gearing of efficiency 65%, calculate the power output of the motor and the current taken by it.

10. A d.c. generator delivers 85A at 120V and is 78% efficient. It is driven at 16 rev/s by a 3-phase 415-V motor of efficiency 82% and power factor (corrected) of 0·9. Calculate the line current to the motor and its shaft torque.

TRANSFORMERS ETC

References: **E.m.f. equation.**   **Ratio and proportion.**
           Phasor Diagrams.   **Phasor resolution and**
           No-load current.   **combination.**
           Efficiency.   **Open and short**
           System short-circuit   **circuit tests.**
           conditions.   **Regulation**

E.m.f. equation

The e.m.f. of a transformer is given by

$$E = 4·44 \times f \times \Phi_{max} \times N$$

where f is the frequency (Hz)

      Φ_{max} is the maximum value of core flux (Wb)

      E is the e.m.f. induced in the winding having N turns (V)

Thus for the primary

$E_P = 4·44 \times f \times \Phi_{max} \times N_P$ where E_P, N_P, E_S, N_S, refer to
and for the secondary   primary and secondary respec-
$E_S = 4·44 \times f \times \Phi_{max} \times N_S$ tively

In each case the e.m.f. and the terminal voltage are equal if the winding resistance and reactance are ignored.

Examples

A. Calculate the maximum value of flux in the core of a transformer having 2000 primary turns and supplied at 240V, 50 Hz.

$$E_P = 4·44 \times f \times \Phi_{max} \times N_P$$
$$240 = 4·44 \times 50 \times \Phi_{max} \times 2000$$
$$\Phi_{max} = \frac{240}{4·44 \times 50 \times 2000}$$
$$= \underline{0·000\ 541\ Wb}\ (0·541\ mWb)$$

113

B. If the maximum flux density in the core of transformer of Example A is not to exceed 0·5 T, calculate the cross-sectional area of the core.

$$\Phi_{max} = B_{max} \times A \quad \text{where } B_{max} \text{ is the maximum flux density and } A \text{ is the cross-sectional area of the core (m}^2\text{)}$$

$$0.000\,541 = 0.5 \times A$$

$$A = \frac{0.000\,541}{0.5}$$

$$= \underline{0.00108\ \text{m}^2}$$

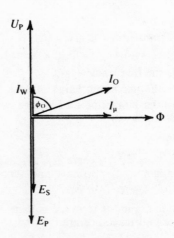

No-load Phasor Diagram

Φ is the flux

E_P and E_S are primary and secondary induced e.m.fs. respectively

U_p is the primary applied voltage

I_0 is the no-load current

I_W and I_μ are its active and reactive components respectively

$\cos\phi_0$ is the no-load (or open-circuit) power factor.

114

C. The no-load current of a 250/50V transformer is 3A at 0·2 p.f. lagging. Draw the no-load phasor diagram accurately to scale and determine the active and reactive components of the no-load current.

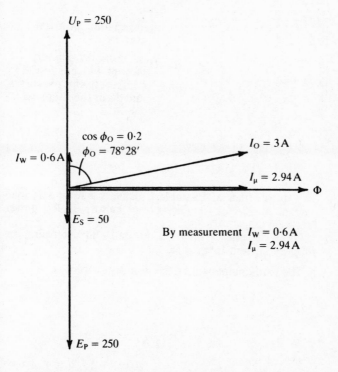

Phasor Diagram on Load (neglecting voltage drops)

115

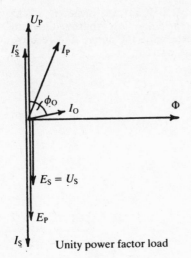

I_S is secondary load current

I_S' is load component of primary current and $I_S' = I_S \times N_S/N_P$

I_0 is no-load primary current

I_P is resultant primary current which is found by combining the phasors I_S' and I_0 in the usual way.

Unity power factor load

D. The transformer of Example C delivers a secondary load current of 30A at (i) unity power factor, (ii) 0·8 power factor lagging.

Draw the phasor diagram on load and determine the primary current in each case.

The load component of the primary current is

$$I_S' = I_S \times \frac{N_S}{N_P}$$

$$= 30 \times \frac{50}{250}$$

(see vol. 2 for transformer ratio problems)

$$= 6A$$

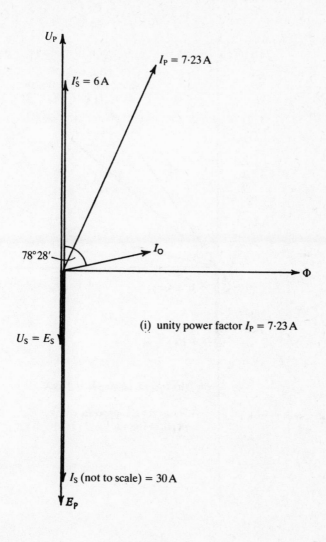

(i) unity power factor $I_P = 7.23$ A

117

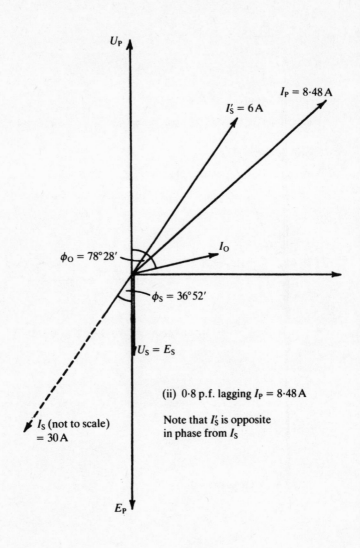

U_P

$I'_S = 6\,\mathrm{A}$

$I_P = 8\cdot48\,\mathrm{A}$

$\phi_O = 78°28'$

I_O

$\phi_S = 36°52'$

$U_S = E_S$

I_S (not to scale) $= 30\,\mathrm{A}$

(ii) 0·8 p.f. lagging $I_P = 8\cdot48\,\mathrm{A}$

Note that I'_S is opposite in phase from I_S

E_P

OPEN-CIRCUIT TEST

E. An open-circuit test on a 15-kVA transformer yielded the following results:

> applied voltage 240V
> current 3A
> power input 144W

Determine the iron loss and magnetising components of the no-load current.

From the phasor diagram of Example C:

$$\frac{I_W}{I_0} = \cos \phi_0 \qquad \text{where } I_W \text{ is the iron-loss component of the open-circuit current } I_0$$

and $\cos \phi_0 = \dfrac{\text{power input}}{\text{VA input}}$

$$= \frac{144}{240 \times 3}$$

$$\therefore \frac{I_W}{3} = \frac{144}{240 \times 3}$$

$$I_W = \frac{144 \times 3}{240 \times 3}$$

$$= \underline{0.6A}$$

also $\dfrac{I_\mu}{I_0} = \sin \phi_0 \qquad$ where I_μ is the magnetising component of I_0

$$\cos \phi_0 = \frac{144}{240 \times 3} = 0.2$$

$$\phi_0 = 78° 28' \quad \sin \phi_0 = 0.9798$$

$$\frac{I_\mu}{3} = 0.9798$$

$$I_\mu = 3 \times 0.9798$$

$$= 2.9394$$

$$= \underline{2.94A}$$

119

or using Pythagoras theorem

$$I_0{}^2 = I_W{}^2 + I_\mu{}^2$$

and
$$I_\mu{}^2 = I_0{}^2 - I_W{}^2 \quad \text{etc.}$$

Short-circuit Test and Efficiency

F. The transformer of Example E circulates full-load current on short circuit when the power input is 200W. Calculate its efficiency at (i) full load, (ii) half load when the power factor is unity in each case.

$$\text{efficiency} = \frac{\text{output}}{\text{input}}$$

$$= \frac{\text{output}}{\text{output} + \text{losses}}$$

(i) the output is 15 kVA at unity power factor = 15 kW.
The full load losses = iron loss + copper loss at full load

$$= 144 + 200$$
$$= 344\text{W}$$

$$\text{efficiency } \eta = \frac{15\,000}{15\,000 + 344}$$

$$= \underline{0{\cdot}978 \text{ or } 97{\cdot}8\%}$$

(ii) Copper loss is proportional to current^2
thus copper loss at half load

$$= (\tfrac{1}{2})^2 \times \text{copper loss at full load}$$
$$= \tfrac{1}{4} \times 200$$
$$= \underline{50\text{W}}$$

Iron losses are constant

$$\text{Thus } \eta = \frac{\tfrac{1}{2} \times 15\,000}{\tfrac{1}{2} \times 15\,000 + 144 + 50}$$

$$= \frac{7500}{7500 + 194}$$

$$= \underline{0{\cdot}975 \text{ or } 97{\cdot}5\%}$$

G. Calculate the full-load efficiency of the transformer of Example F when the load power factor is 0·8 lagging.

$$\text{output} = 15 \text{ kVA at } 0·8 \text{ p.f.}$$

$$= 15 \times 0·8$$

$$= 12 \text{ kW}$$

$$\eta = \frac{12\,000}{12\,000 + 344}$$

$$= \underline{97·2\%}$$

Maximum Efficiency

H. Calculate the value of the load for which the efficiency of the transformer considered will have its maximum value.

At maximum efficiency copper and iron losses are equal.

Let $1/n$ be the fraction of full load at which copper and iron losses are equal, then:

$$\left(\frac{1}{n}\right)^2 \times 200 = 144$$

$$\left(\frac{1}{n}\right)^2 = \frac{144}{200}$$

$$\frac{1}{n} = \sqrt{\frac{144}{200}}$$

$$= \sqrt{0·72}$$

$$= 0·8485$$

Thus maximum efficiency occurs when the load is

$$0·8485 \times 15 = \underline{12·73 \text{ kVA}}$$

All-day Efficiency

All-day efficiency $\eta_D = \dfrac{\text{Energy output}}{\text{Energy input}}$ (over 24 hours)

121

I. The transformer previously considered is energised continuously but is on load of 15 kVA unity power factor for 15 hours only. Calculate its all-day efficiency.

iron-loss energy over 24 hours $= 144 \times 24$

$$= 3456 \text{ Wh} \quad \text{(watt-hour)}$$

full-load copper-loss energy over 15 hours $= 200 \times 15$

$$= 3000 \text{ Wh}$$

output energy $= 15\,000 \times 15$

$$= 225\,000 \text{ Wh}$$

$$\eta_D = \frac{225\,000}{225\,000 + 3000 + 3456}$$

$$= 0.972 \text{ or } 97.2\%$$

Regulation

Percentage regulation

$$= \frac{\text{change in secondary voltage from no load to full load}}{\text{open-circuit secondary voltage}} \times 100$$

J. Calculate the full-load terminal voltage of a transformer having 5% regulation and open-circuit secondary voltage 400V

change in voltage $= \dfrac{5}{100} \times 400$

$$= 20\text{V}$$

Terminal voltage on full load

$$= 400 - 20$$

$$= 380\text{V}$$

K. A transformer has a no-load and full-load secondary voltage of 500V and 487V respectively. Calculate the percentage regulation of the transformer.

122

Percentage regulation $= \dfrac{U_s \text{(no-load)} - U_s \text{(on-load)}}{U_s \text{(no-load)}} \times 100$

$$= \frac{500 - 487}{500} \times 100$$

$$= \frac{13}{500} \times 100$$

$$= 2 \cdot 6\%$$

System Short Circuit conditions

L. A factory generating station employs parallel connected three-phase generators and transformers as shown below. Calculate the short-circuit MVA and the short circuit current in the event of a short circuit at switchgear positions:

    A when switchgear B is in open condition and generator X operating

    B when switchgear A is in open condition and generator Y operating

    C when both switchgear A and B are in closed condition and both generators operating

Ignore the impedance of the interconnecting cables.

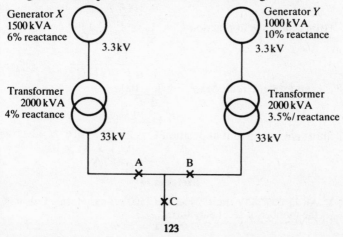

Take a 1 MVA base.

L.H. Generator $\dfrac{6 \times 1}{1 \cdot 5} = 4\%$ reactance

L.H. Transformer $\dfrac{4 \times 1}{2} = 2\%$ reactance

∴ Total reactance L.H. branch $= 4 + 2 = 6\%$

Short circuit MVA at position A $= \dfrac{1 \times 100}{6}$

$$= 16 \cdot 6 \text{ MVA.}$$

Short circuit current at position A. $= \dfrac{16 \cdot 6 \times 10^6}{\sqrt{3} \times 33 \times 10^3}$

$$= \underline{290 \cdot 4 \text{ A}}$$

R.H. Generator $\dfrac{10 \times 1}{1} = 10\%$ reactance

R.H. Transformer $\dfrac{3 \cdot 5 \times 1}{2} = 1 \cdot 75\%$ reactance

∴ Total reactance R.H. Branch $= 10 + 1 \cdot 75 = 11 \cdot 75\%$

Short circuit MVA at position B $= \dfrac{1 \times 100}{11 \cdot 75}$

$$= 8 \cdot 5 \text{ MVA.}$$

Short circuit current at position B $= \dfrac{8 \cdot 5 \times 10^6}{\sqrt{3} \times 33 \times 10^6}$

$$= \underline{148 \cdot 7 \text{ A}}$$

Total reactance at position C $= \dfrac{1}{X} = \dfrac{1}{X_1} + \dfrac{1}{X_2}$

$$= \dfrac{1}{X} = \dfrac{1}{6} + \dfrac{1}{11 \cdot 75} = 3 \cdot 97\%$$

and short circuit MVA $= \dfrac{1 \times 100}{3 \cdot 97}$

$$= \underline{25 \cdot 19 \text{ MVA}}$$

Short circuit current at position C $= \dfrac{25 \cdot 19 \times 10^6}{\sqrt{3} \times 33 \times 10^3}$

$$= \underline{440 \cdot 7 \text{A}}$$

Exercises 13

1. An 11 000/240V transformer has 1500 primary turns. Calculate the number of secondary turns.

124

from the graph the value of load at which the transformer has its maximum efficiency and calculate the copper loss at this value of load.

12. (a) Explain the differences between a single-phase double-wound transformer and a single-phase auto-transformer.
    What are the requirements of the I.E.E. Regulations regarding the use of auto-transformers?

    (b) A 40-kVA single-phase transformer was tested for efficiency by the 'open-circuit' and 'short-circuit' tests. On short circuit, at full-load current, the power used was 1140W. On open circuit, the power used was 800W.
    Calculate the efficiency of the transformer at unity power factor on (i) full load, and (ii) half full load.   (C & G)

13. (a) Why is it usually necessary to cool transformers? Describe briefly two methods by which this can be done.

    (b) A 20-kVA transformer when tested was found to have 600 watts iron losses, and 700 watts copper losses when supplying full load at unity power factor.
    Calculate the efficiency of the transformer at unity power factor (i) on full load, (ii) on half load.   (C & G)

14. The full-load copper and iron losses of a 50-kVA transformer are respectively 250W and 150W. Calculate the efficiency of the transformer on (i) full load, (ii) half load, when the load power factor is 0·8 lagging in each case.

15. (a) Explain why transformers need to be cooled.

    (b) A 600-kVA 3-phase transformer is immersed in a tank containing $2\,m^3$ of insulating oil. The efficiency of the transformer at full load is 97 per cent.
    Calculate the average rise in temperature in degC of the oil after a 3-hour run at full load and unity power factor, assuming that 60 per cent of the heat energy lost in the transformer is expended in heating the oil.

    Specific heat of oil 2135 J/(kg degC).
    $1\,m^3$ of oil weighs 900 kg.   (C & G)

16. A 25-kVA transformer has iron loss 500W and full-load copper loss 650W. Determine the value of unity power factor load at which the efficiency will have its maximum value and calculate that value.

17. A 20-kVA transformer operates with maximum efficiency of 98% when on 0·9 of its full load at unity power factor. Calculate its efficiency at full load.

2. Calculate the primary current of a 6600/400V transformer when its secondary current is 200A.

3. A transformer for 50 Hz working has 1500 primary turns, 650 secondary turns, the cross-sectional area of the core is 1500 mm², and the maximum flux density is 0·75 T. Calculate the primary and secondary e.m.f.

4. A 240/12V 50-Hz transformer has 2000 primary turns and the cross-sectional area of the core is 1000 mm². Calculate the maximum value of flux density in the core.

5. The primary supply voltage of a transformer is 500V at 50 Hz. The cross-sectional area of the core is 2500 mm². Calculate the number of primary turns in order that the maximum value of flux density shall not exceed 0·75 T.

6. If the secondary voltage of the transformer of question 5 is to be 2000V, calculate the number of secondary turns.

7. The magnetising and iron-loss components of a 240/120V transformer are respectively 5A and 2A. Draw the no-load phasor diagram accurately to scale and determine from it the no-load current and power factor.

8. The no-load current of a transformer is 4A at 0·2 power factor lagging. Determine graphically or calculate the magnetising and iron-loss components of the no-load current.

9. An open-circuit test on a 5-kVA transformer yielded the following results:
   Primary voltage 240V; Primary current 2A; Power input 86·4W.
   Calculate the magnetising and iron-loss components of the no-load current.

10. The magnetising and loss components of the no-load current of an 11 000/240V transformer are respectively 2·5A and 0·5A. By means of an accurately constructed phasor diagram or otherwise determine the primary current when the secondary current is 100A at:

    (i) unity power factor;
    (ii) 0·8 power factor lagging;
    (iii) 0·8 power factor leading.

11. Calculate the efficiency of the transformer of question 9 for a range of values of load at unity power factor up to full load. Plot a graph of efficiency against the fraction of full load. State

18. A 15-kVA transformer has iron loss 100W and full-load copper loss 125W. It is energised continuously and supplies the following loads over a 24-hour period:

    from 0800 to 1800 hours 8 kVA at unity power factor;
    from 1600 to 2400 hours 6 kVA at 0·8 power factor lagging.

    Calculate the all-day efficiency.

19. A 100-kVA transformer has ordinary efficiency 98% on full-load unity power factor when its iron and copper losses may be taken as equal. Over a period of 24 hours it supplies loads as follows:

    0000 to 1200 hours 40 kW at unity power factor;
    0200 to 2200 hours 35 kVA at 0·75 power factor lagging.

    Calculate its all-day efficiency.

20. The open-circuit voltage of a transformer is 415V. On full load, the terminal voltage is 400V. Calculate the percentage regulation.

21. A 240V transformer has 5% regulation. Calculate its terminal voltage on full load.

22. Using the diagram from example L. The transformer X is replaced by a new 2000 kVA transformer having a reactance of 5%. Calculate the new short circuit MVA and short circuit current at switchgear position A and position C.

R

ELECTROSTATICS

References: **Electric field.**
           Field strength.
           Flux density.
           Parallel plate capacitor.
           Series and parallel arrangement of capacitors.
           Quantity of charge and energy stored.
           Charging and discharging curves.

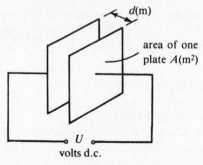

An arrangement of two parallel metal plates each having cross-sectional area A (m^2) and separated by insulation of thickness d (m) is called a capacitor. When it is connected to a d.c. supply of U volts it becomes charged. The following facts are known:

1. The quantity of charge in coulombs is

$$Q = CU \text{ where } C \text{ is the capacitance (farad)}$$

2. The electric field strength

$$E = U/d \text{ (volts/metre)}$$

3. The electric flux density

$$D = Q/A \quad \text{(coulomb/metre}^2\text{)}$$

4. The energy stored

$$W = \tfrac{1}{2} CU^2 \text{ (joule)}$$

5. The capacitance of the arrangement is

$$C = \epsilon_0 \epsilon_r \frac{A}{d} \quad \text{(farad) where } \epsilon_0 \text{ is the permittivity}$$
of free space with numerical value $8 \cdot 85 \times 10^{-12}$

ϵ_r is the relative permittivity of the insulator or dielectric.

Examples

A. Two parallel metal plates each of area $0 \cdot 01$ m^2 and separated by a layer of mica 2 mm thick and of relative permittivity 6 are connected to a 100-V d.c. supply.

Calculate:
   (a) the capacitance of the arrangement;
   (b) the charge stored;
   (c) the energy stored;
   (d) the field strength in the dielectric;
   (e) the electric flux density.

(a) $C = \epsilon_0\epsilon_r \dfrac{A}{d}$

$$= 8\cdot85 \times 10^{-12} \times 6 \times 0\cdot01 \times \frac{1}{2/1000}$$

$$= 265\cdot5 \times 10^{-12} \quad \text{farad}$$

$$= \underline{265\cdot5} \ (\text{pF}) \ \text{picofarad}$$

$$(1\text{F} = 10^6 \ \mu\text{F}$$

$$= 10^{12} \ \text{pF})$$

(b) $Q = CU$

$$= 265\cdot5 \times 10^{-12} \times 100$$

$$= 26\,550 \times 10^{-12} \quad \text{coulomb}$$

$$= 0\cdot02655 \times 10^{-6} \quad \text{coulomb}$$

$$= \underline{0\cdot02655} \ \text{microcoulomb} \quad (\mu\text{C})$$

(c) $W = \frac{1}{2} CU^2$

$$= \tfrac{1}{2} \times 265\cdot5 \times 100^2 \times 10^{-12}$$

$$= 132\cdot75 \times 10^{-8} \quad \text{joule}$$

$$= 1\cdot3275 \times 10^{-6} \quad \text{joule}$$

$$= \underline{1\cdot3275} \ \text{microjoule} \ (\mu\text{J})$$

(d) $E = \dfrac{U}{d}$

$$= \frac{100}{2/1000}$$

$$= \underline{50\,000} \ \text{volts/metre}$$

(e) $D = Q/A$

$$= \frac{0\cdot02655 \times 10^{-6}}{0\cdot01}$$

$$= \underline{0\cdot02655 \times 10^{-4}} \ \text{coulomb/metre}^2$$

Series Arrangement of Capacitors

If a number of capacitors of values C_1, C_2, C_3, etc. are connected in series they are equivalent to a single capacitor of value C given by

$$\frac{1}{C} = \frac{1}{C_1} + \frac{1}{C_2} + \frac{1}{C_3} \quad \text{etc.}$$

When the arrangement is connected to a d.c. supply of U volts the charge stored is the same on each and equal to $Q = CU$.

B. Calculate the value of a capacitor which when connected in series with another of $20 \, \mu F$ will give a resulting capacitance of $12 \, \mu F$.

$$\frac{1}{C} = \frac{1}{C_1} + \frac{1}{C_2}$$

$$\frac{1}{12} = \frac{1}{20} + \frac{1}{C_2}$$

$$\frac{1}{C_2} = \frac{1}{12} - \frac{1}{20}$$

$$\frac{1}{C_2} = \frac{5-3}{60}$$

$$= \frac{2}{60}$$

$$C_2 = \frac{60}{2} = 30 \, \mu F$$

The required value is thus $30 \, \mu F$

C. Capacitors of 4 μF, 6 μF and 12 μF are connected in series to a 300-V d.c. supply. Calculate:

(a) The equivalent single capacitor;
(b) The charge stored on each capacitor;
(c) The p.d. across each capacitor;
(d) The energy stored in each capacitor.

(a) $$\frac{1}{C} = \frac{1}{4} + \frac{1}{6} + \frac{1}{12}$$

$$= \frac{3+2+1}{12}$$

$$= \frac{6}{12}$$

$$C = \frac{12}{6} = \underline{2\,\mu F}$$

(b) Charge stored on each = charge stored on equivalent single capacitor

$$Q = CU$$

$$= 2 \times 300$$

$$= \underline{600\,\mu C} \quad \text{(microcoulomb because capacitance is in microfarad).}$$

(c) The p.d. on each capacitor is found by using the formula $Q = CU$ where C is the appropriate value of capacitance and Q is as calculated above.

Rearranging the formula gives

$$U = \frac{Q}{C}$$

Thus for the 4-μF capacitor

$$U_4 = \frac{600}{4} = \underline{150V}$$

Similarly

$$U_6 = \frac{600}{6} = \underline{100V}$$

and $$U_{12} = \frac{600}{12} = \underline{50V}$$

(Note that these sum to 300V)

(d) The energy stored is calculated by using the formula $W = \frac{1}{2}CU^2$ with the appropriate capacitance and voltage calculated above.

Thus for the 4-μF capacitor

$$W_4 = \frac{1}{2} \times \frac{4}{10^6} \times (150)^2$$

$$= \underline{0 \cdot 045 \text{ J}}$$

$$W_6 = \frac{1}{2} \times \frac{6}{10^6} \times (100)^2$$

$$= \underline{0 \cdot 03 \text{ J}}$$

and $\quad W_{12} = \frac{1}{2} \times \frac{12}{10^6} \times (50)^2$

$$= \underline{0 \cdot 015 \text{ J}}$$

Parallel Arrangement of Capacitors

If a number of capacitors of values C_1, C_2, C_3, etc. are connected in parallel they are equivalent to a single capacitor of value C given by

$$C = C_1 + C_2 + C_3 \quad \text{etc.}$$

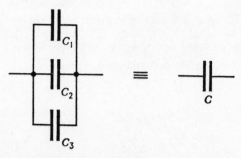

When the arrangement is connected to a d.c. supply of U volts the total charge is the sum of the charges stored separately on each, i.e. if Q be the total charge

$$Q = Q_1 + Q_2 + Q_3$$

where Q_1 is the charge on C_1 etc. and $Q_1 = C_1 U$ etc.
The voltage U is common to all the capacitors.

D. Capacitors of $4\,\mu F$ and $5\,\mu F$ are connected in parallel and charged to 20V. Calculate the charge stored on each and the total stored energy.

The p.d. is the same on each capacitor, the charge on the $4\text{-}\mu F$ capacitor is

$$Q_4 = C_4 U$$
$$= 4 \times 20$$
$$= \underline{80\,\mu C} \quad \text{(microcoulombs because } C \text{ is in microfarads)}$$

similarly

$$Q_5 = C_5 U$$
$$= 5 \times 20$$
$$= \underline{100\,\mu C}$$

The total energy may be calculated either by finding the energy stored separately on each capacitor and summing or by considering the total capacitance thus:

$$C = 4 + 5$$
$$= 9\,\mu F$$

and total energy

$$W = \tfrac{1}{2} C U^2$$
$$= \tfrac{1}{2} \times 9 \times 20^2$$
$$= \underline{1800\,\mu J} \quad \text{(microjoules because } C \text{ is in microfarads)}$$

E. Calculate the value of a single capacitor equivalent to the arrangement shown.

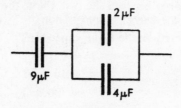

The capacitor equivalent to the parallel group

$$= 2 + 4$$
$$= 6 \, \mu\text{F}$$

The circuit then reduces to

9μF   6μF

and the equivalent capacitor of value C is given by

$$\frac{1}{C} = \frac{1}{9} + \frac{1}{6}$$
$$= \frac{2 + 3}{18}$$
$$C = \frac{18}{5} = \underline{3 \cdot 6 \, \mu\text{F}}$$

F. A capacitor of 10 μF is fully charged from a 100-V d.c. supply and immediately connected to an uncharged capacitor of 15 μF. Calculate (a) the energy stored initially in the 10-μF capacitor and (b) the total energy stored subsequently in the two capacitors.

Initial energy stored
$$\begin{aligned} W_1 &= \tfrac{1}{2}CU^2 \\ &= \tfrac{1}{2} \times 10 \times (100)^2 \\ &= 50\,000 \, \mu\text{J} \\ &= \underline{0 \cdot 05 \, \text{J}} \end{aligned} \qquad (a)$$

Subsequently the capacitors are effectively connected in parallel and the charge initially on the 10-μF capacitor is then shared between the two. (Note the total *charge* is constant, the *energy* stored is not.)

Charge stored on the 10-μF capacitor
$$\begin{aligned} Q &= CU \\ &= 10 \times 100 \\ &= 1000 \, \mu\text{C} \end{aligned}$$

134

The two capacitors in parallel are equivalent to a single one of value $10 + 15 = 25\ \mu F$

The common p.d. on the two capacitors is found by using the formula $Q = CU$

Thus $$1000\ \mu C = 25\ \mu F \times U$$

$$U = 40V$$

The final energy stored $W_2 = \frac{1}{2} \times 25 \times (40)^2$

$$= 20\ 000\ \mu J$$

$$= \underline{0 \cdot 02\ J} \qquad (b)$$

The difference between (a) and (b) is the energy dissipated during the sharing of the charge between the two capacitors.

The Multiplate Capacitor

An arrangement of n parallel plates each of effective area A (m²) and separated by insulation of thickness d (m) and of relative permittivity ϵ_r produces $(n-1)$ capacitors in parallel and the capacitance of the arrangement is

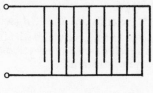

$$C = (n-1)\ \epsilon_0 \epsilon_r \frac{A}{d}\ \ F$$

G. A parallel plate capacitor has 21 semicircular plates each of diameter 5 cm. The plates are 2 mm apart in air. Calculate the capacitance of the arrangement.

$$C = (n-1)\ \epsilon_0 \epsilon_r \frac{A}{d}$$

$$= (21-1) \times \frac{8 \cdot 85}{10^{12}} \times 1 \times \frac{1}{2} \times \frac{\pi}{4} \times \frac{5^2}{10^4} \times \frac{1}{2/1000}\ \ F$$

(i) the relative permittivity of air is taken to be 1,

(ii) the formula for the area of a circle of diameter d is $\pi d^2/4$, the area of a semicircle is one half of this,

(iii) the conversions of square centimetres to square metres and millimetres to metres.

$$C = 20 \times \frac{8\cdot85}{10^{12}} \times \frac{1}{2} \times \frac{\pi}{4} \times \frac{5^2}{10^4} \times \frac{1000}{2} \times 10^{12} \text{ pF}$$

$$= \underline{86\cdot9 \text{ pF}}$$

d.c. excited circuit having resistance and capacitance in series

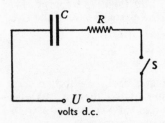

If such a circuit having capacitance C farad in series with resistance R ohms is supplied at U volts d.c., the voltage on the capacitor at any instant t seconds after closing the switch S is found as follows:

(1) The final value of the voltage on the capacitor is U, the supply voltage.

(2) Calculate the time constant $T = CR$ (seconds).

(3) Draw graph axes to suitable scales (the time required for the voltage to reach its maximum value may be taken as five times the time constant).

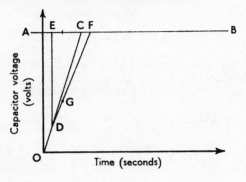

(4) Draw the horizontal line AB so that OA = *U*. Mark AC = *T*. Join OC. Select any point D on OC near to O. Project upwards vertically from D to E on AB. Mark EF = *T*. Join FD. Repeat the procedure for a new point G on DF and so on until the complete curve is traced.

During the charging of the capacitor the current decays in a manner illustrated graphically as follows.

1. Calculate the initial value of the current

$$I = U/R$$

2. The time constant is as before

$$T = CR$$

3. Draw graph axes to suitable scales.

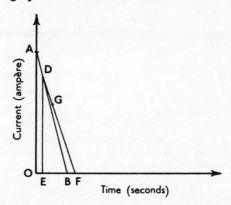

4. Mark OA = *I* and OB = *T*. Join AB and select any point D on AB close to A. Project from D to E on the time axis and mark EF = *T*. Join DF. Select a new point G on DF and repeat the procedure until a complete curve is traced.

When a capacitor of value *C* farad has been fully charged to *U* volts and is then discharged through a resistor of *R* ohms, curves showing the decay of both capacitor voltage and current are constructed in exactly the same way as that described above.

H. A capacitor of 20 μF and a resistor of 5 MΩ are connected in series to a d.c. supply of 100V. Determine graphically, for the instant when the switch has been closed for 3 minutes

(a) the p.d. on the capacitor;

(b) the charge and energy stored in the capacitor;

(c) the charging current.

For (a) and (b) the curve shown is required.

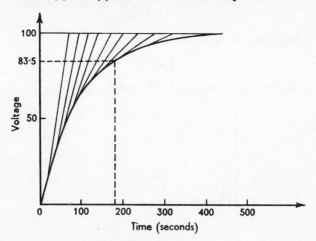

Time constant $T = CR$

$$= 5 \times 10^6 \times \frac{20}{10^6}$$

$$= 100 \text{ seconds}$$

From the curve at $t = 180$ seconds

Capacitor voltage $U_c = \underline{83 \cdot 5 \text{V}}$ **(a)**

The charge $Q = CU_c$

$$= \frac{20}{10^6} \times 83 \cdot 5$$

$$= 167 \, \mu\text{C} \quad \text{(microcoulomb)}$$

138

The energy
$$W = \tfrac{1}{2}CU_c^2$$
$$= \tfrac{1}{2} \times \frac{20}{10^6} \times (83{\cdot}5)^2$$
$$= \underline{0{\cdot}0697\,\text{J}} \qquad\qquad (b)$$

(c) may be determined by constructing the curve showing the decay of current in the manner described or by using Kirchhoff's law for the voltages acting in the circuit, for the p.d. across the resistor is $i \times R$ where i is the current at the instant considered

and
$$U = U_c + i \times R$$
$$100 = 83{\cdot}5 + i \times 5 \times 10^6$$
$$i \times 5 \times 10^6 = 100 - 83{\cdot}5$$
$$= 16{\cdot}5$$
$$i = \frac{16{\cdot}5}{5 \times 10^6}\,\text{A}$$
$$= \frac{16{\cdot}5 \times 10^6}{5 \times 10^6}\,\mu\text{A} \quad \text{(micro ampère)}$$
$$i = \underline{3{\cdot}3\,\mu\text{A}} \qquad\qquad (c)$$

Exercises 14

$$(\epsilon_0 = 8{\cdot}85 \times 10^{-12})$$

1. A capacitor consists of two parallel metal plates each 100 mm by 120 mm and separated by a sheet of insulation having relative permittivity 7·5 and of thickness 1·5 mm. Calculate:
   (a) its capacitance;
   (b) the charge and energy stored when the capacitor is charged to 75V;
   (c) the electric flux density and voltage gradient under these conditions.

2. Calculate the diameter of circular plates required to produce a capacitance of 100 pF if the plates are separated by 0·5 mm of insulation of relative permittivity 5.

3. A capacitor of 100 pF is charged to a p.d. of 100V. Calculate the charge and energy stored. Calculate also the energy stored if the distance between the plates be (a) halved, (b) doubled.

   (Remember that the charge (Q) stored is constant, both C and U vary.)

4. Capacitors of 3 μF and 5 μF are connected in series to a 240-V d.c. supply. Calculate:

   (a) the resultant capacitance;
   (b) the charge on each;
   (c) the p.d. on each;
   (d) the energy stored in each.

5. Calculate the value of a single capacitor equivalent to three 24-μF capacitors connected in series. What would be the value of 10 such capacitors connected in series?

6. What value of capacitor connected in series with one of 20 μF will produce a resultant capacitance of 15 μF?

7. Three capacitors of values 8 μF, 12 μF, and 16 μF respectively are connected across a 240-V d.c. supply (i) in series, and (ii) in parallel. Calculate in each case, the resultant capacitance, and also the potential difference across each capacitor.

   (C & G part question)

8. Calculate the value of the single capacitor equivalent to the arrangement shown.

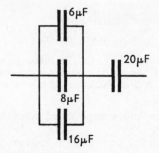

9. Capacitors of 12 μF and 20 μF are connected in parallel. A third capacitor of 64 μF is connected in series with these two in parallel and the whole circuit is supplied with 300V d.c. Calculate the charge and the energy stored in each capacitor.

10. A capacitor of 60 μF is fully charged from a 200-V d.c. supply and then connected to an uncharged capacitor of 40 μF. Calculate:

   (a) the charge and energy stored initially in the 60-μF capacitor;

   (b) the potential difference and the energy stored in the combination.

   Account for the difference in the values of energy stored.

11. A multiplate capacitor consists of 25 plates each of area 600 mm². The plates are separated in air by a distance of 0·5 mm. Calculate the capacitance of the capacitor.

12. The 12 plates of a multiplate capacitor are semi-circular and 40 mm in diameter. They are fixed so that adjacent plates are 0·75 mm apart in air. Calculate the capacitance of the arrangement.

13. A 60-μF capacitor is charged from a 100-V d.c. supply through a 0·5 MΩ resistor. Construct a curve showing:

   (a) charging current plotted against time;

   (b) the capacitor voltage plotted against time.

14. A 10-μF capacitor having been charged to 340V is discharged through a 5 MΩ resistor. Construct a curve showing the capacitor voltage plotted against time.

15. The following results were obtained when a capacitor of unknown value was charged to 150V and then discharged through a 5 MΩ resistor. If the time constant (CR) is equal to the time required, from the commencement of the discharge, for the current in the circuit to fall to 0·368 of its maximum value, estimate the value of the capacitor.

Time after discharge commences (s)	10	20	30	50	60	70	80
current (μA)	23·6	18·6	15·0	9·5	7·5	6·2	5·0

Time after discharge commences (s)	90	100	120	130	150	200	250
current (μA)	4·0	3·0	2·0	1·5	0·7	0·3	0

UTILISATION OF ELECTRIC POWER II
ILLUMINATION

References: **Illumination terms and measurement.**
Point-by-point lighting calculations using the inverse square law and cosine law.

Inverse Square Law

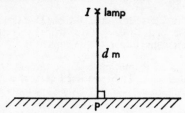

A lamp of luminous intensity I candela in all directions below the horizontal when suspended d metres above a surface, produces illumination at P below the lamp given by

$$E_P = \frac{I}{d^2} \text{ lumen per square metre or lux (lx)}$$

Cosine Law

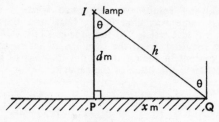

Figure A

The illumination at any other point Q, x metres from P and on the same horizontal plane through P is given by

$$E_Q = \frac{I}{h^2} \cos \theta \text{ lx}$$

where h and θ are as shown on the diagram

also $$h^2 = d^2 + x^2 \quad \text{(Pythagoras)}$$

and $$\cos \theta = \frac{d}{h}$$

$$= \frac{d}{\sqrt{d^2 + x^2}}$$

Examples

A. A luminaire producing luminous intensity 1500 candela in all directions below the horizontal is suspended 4m above the floor. Calculate the illumination produced at a point P immediately below the luminaire and at a point Q 2·5m away from P.

The situation is as illustrated in figure A.

The illumination at P

$$E_P = \frac{1500}{4^2}$$

$$= \underline{93·75 \text{ lx}}$$

The illumination at Q

$$E_Q = \frac{1500}{22·25} \times \frac{4}{4·717}$$

h and d being calculated as shown above

$$= \underline{57·2 \text{ lx}}$$

The illumination at a point due to a number of luminaires is found by calculating the illumination due to each luminaire separately and then adding to find the resultant.

B. An area is 16m square and is illuminated by four luminaires, one mounted at each corner at a height of 6m. The luminaires each have luminous intensity 1000 cd in all directions below the horizontal. Calculate the illumination produced at the centre of the square.

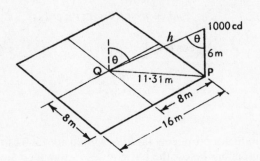

The diagram shows the situation as far as a single luminaire is concerned. In order to calculate $\cos \phi$ it is first necessary to determine the length PQ where Q is at the centre of the square.

By Pythagoras $PQ^2 = 8^2 + 8^2$

$$= 128$$

and $PQ = 11 \cdot 31 \, \text{m}$

as before $\cos \theta = \dfrac{6}{\sqrt{(6^2 + 11 \cdot 31^2)}}$

$$= \dfrac{6}{12 \cdot 81}$$

also $h^2 = 6^2 + 11 \cdot 31^2$

$$= 164$$

The illumination due to one luminaire

$$= \dfrac{1000}{164} \times \dfrac{6}{12 \cdot 81}$$

$$= 2 \cdot 856 \, \text{lx}$$

The total illumination

$$= 4 \times 2 \cdot 856$$

$$= \underline{11 \cdot 42 \, \text{lx}}$$

Exercises 15

1. A luminaire emitting 250 cd in all directions is fixed 4m above a horizontal surface. Calculate the level of illumination at (i) a point P on the surface vertically beneath the luminaire and (ii) a point Q 3m away from P.

2. Two luminaires illuminate a passage way. The luminaires are 12m apart, each emits 240 cd and is 3m above the floor. Calculate the illumination at a point on the floor midway between the luminaires.

3. Determine the level of illumination at a point vertically beneath one of the luminaires in question 2.

4. A square area 10m by 10m is illuminated by four luminaires. Each luminaire is mounted on a pole 7·5m high at one corner of the square and emits 1050 cd in all directions. Determine the level of illumination at points:

   (a) at the centre of the square;
   (b) at the foot of one pole;
   (c) midway along one of the sides of the square.

5. An advertisement board, 5m square, is fixed to a wall with the bottom edge near the ground. A luminaire, giving a luminous intensity of 4000 candelas in all directions towards the board, is fixed level with the bottom of the board, and 6m distant, giving maximum illumination at the centre of the bottom edge.

   Calculate the illumination:
   (a) at the centre of the bottom edge;
   (b) at the centre of the top edge;
   (c) at one of the top corners.

   Suggest a method of giving reasonably even illumination over the whole board.   ˙(C & G)

6. A luminaire is suspended 2m above a level workbench, such that the luminous intensity in all directions below the horizontal is 400 candelas.

   Calculate the illumination at a point A on the surface of the bench immediately below the luminaire, and at other bench positions 1m, 2m and 3m from A in a straight line.

                                                        (C & G)

7. Two luminaires are suspended 2m apart, and 2·5m above a level workbench. The luminaires are such that each has a luminous intensity of 200 candle-power (candelas) in all directions below the horizontal.

Calculate the total illumination at bench level, immediately below each luminaire and midway between them.

Describe briefly an instrument you could use to check the illumination in such a case. Explain how it works.   (C & G)

8. A square area, 20m by 20m, is to be illuminated by four luminaires, one at each corner each mounted on a pole 8m high. The level of illumination required at the centre of the square is 10 lx. Calculate the luminous intensity required of each luminaire.

UTILISATION OF ELECTRIC POWER III
ILLUMINATION

References: **Illumination terms and measurement.**
Utilisation factor.
Maintenance factor.
Lumen method.
Interior lighting systems.

$$\frac{\text{Total}}{\text{luminous flux}} = \frac{\text{Service value of illumination} \times \text{area}}{\text{Utilisation factor} \times \text{maintenance factor}}$$

where the illumination is given in lux and the area is measured in square metres.

Examples

A. Estimate the total luminous flux required to provide a service value of 120 1x in a room 5m by 7m. Utilisation and maintenance factors are respectively 0·6 and 0·8.

Substituting the values in the formula:

$$\text{Total luminous flux} = \frac{120 \times 5 \times 7}{0·6 \times 0·8}$$

$$= \underline{8750 \text{ lm}}$$

B. Calculate the total power required for the installation of example A if the luminaires used have a efficacy of 12 lumens per watt.

$$\text{Power} = \frac{\text{total lumens}}{\text{lumens per watt}}$$

$$= \frac{8750}{12} \frac{\text{lm}}{\text{lm/W}}$$

$$= \underline{729\text{W}}$$

Spacing-Height Ratio

For a regular square arrangement of fittings this is

$$\frac{\text{distance between adjacent luminaires}}{\text{height of luminaires above the working plane}}$$

C. Estimate a suitable spacing between luminaires which have a spacing height ratio of 1·5 and are suspended 4m above the working plane.

If S be the spacing and H the height

$$\frac{S}{H} = 1\cdot5$$

$$S = 1\cdot5 \times 4$$

$$= \underline{6\text{m}}$$

D. A hall, 15m by 20m, is to be illuminated to a level of 70 lx. Luminaires having an efficacy of 12 1m/W and spacing-height ratio 1·2 are to be suspended 4m above the floor. Estimate the number of luminaires required and the power of each luminaire. Assume a utilisation factor 0·5 and a maintenance factor of 0·8.

Total lumens required from all luminaires

$$= \frac{\text{lux} \times \text{area}}{\text{utilisation factor} \times \text{maintenance factor}}$$

$$= \frac{70 \times 15 \times 20}{0\cdot5 \times 0\cdot8}$$

$$= \underline{52\,500\text{ lm}}$$

147

Next find the distance between adjacent luminaires.

$$\frac{S}{H} = 1 \cdot 2$$

$$\therefore \ S = 1 \cdot 2 \times 4$$

$$= \underline{4 \cdot 8m}$$

The number of rows of luminaires

$$= \frac{\text{width of room}}{\text{spacing}}$$

$$= \frac{15m}{4 \cdot 8m}$$

$$= \underline{3 \text{ say}}$$

The number of luminaires per row

$$= \frac{\text{length of room}}{\text{spacing}}$$

$$= \frac{20}{4 \cdot 8}$$

$$= \underline{4 \text{ say}}$$

Total number of luminaires

$$= 4 \times 3$$

$$= \underline{12}$$

Lumens per luminaire $= \dfrac{52\ 500}{12}$

$$= \underline{4375 \text{ lm}}$$

Watts per luminaire $= \dfrac{4375 \ \text{lm}}{12 \ \text{lm/W}}$

$$= \underline{364 \cdot 6W}$$

300W luminaires will probably suffice.

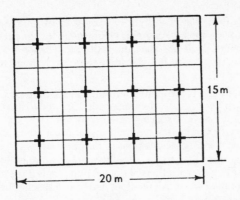

15 m

20 m

A scale plan of the room can be drawn to show the positions of the luminaires.

Exercises 16

1. A circular assembly hall 15m in diameter is to be illuminated to a general level of 200 lx. Utilisation and maintenance factors may be taken as 0·6 and 0·8 respectively. Estimate the power required to illuminate the hall:

   (a) using tungsten luminaires having an efficacy of 14 lm/W;
   (b) using fluorescent luminaires having an efficacy of 40 lm/W.

2. A workshop is 9m by 20m. An illumination of 200 lx is required and this is to be obtained by using luminaires with an efficacy of 40 lm/W. The utilisation factor may be taken as 0·45 and a maintenance factor of 0·7 should be allowed. Calculate:

   (a) the power required;
   (b) the cost of the energy used in a month of 20 days if the charge is on the basis of 8p per unit for the first 60 units and 5p for each additional unit, and the lighting is in use 4 hours per day.

3. A room 7m by 10m is to be used as a general office and must be provided with illumination to a level of 400 lx. 150W luminaires are to be installed giving a utilisation factor 0·5 and requiring a maintenance factor of 0·8. Assuming that the efficacy of the luminaires is 13 lm/W, calculate the number of luminaires required.

4. Describe one form of portable instrument for measuring values of illumination in different parts of a room.

An office, 30m long by 15m wide, is to be illuminated to an intensity of 400 lx. Assuming the average lumen output of the luminaires is 30 per watt, the utilisation factor 0·5, and the maintenance factor 0·8, calculate the total wattage required.

(C & G)

5. A church hall is 40m long and 14m wide. It is to be illuminated by a number of luminaires suspended 3m above the floor. The luminaires have a spacing-height ratio of 1·75. Estimate the number of luminaires required and draw a scale plan of the building marking the positions of the luminaires.

6. Draw a scale plan of an office 20m long and 6m wide to show the number and positions of the lighting points if the luminaires are mounted 4m above the floor and have a spacing-height ratio of 1·8.

7. A light assembly shop, 17m long, 8m wide and 3m to trusses, is to be illuminated to a level of 200 lx. The utilisation and maintenance factors are respectively 0·54 and 0·8. Make a scale drawing of the plan of the shop and set out the required lighting points, assuming the use of tungsten luminaires. You may assume an efficacy of 13 lm/W. (C & G)

8. A room 28m by 7m is provided with sixteen 300W luminaires having an efficacy of 13 lm/W. Assuming a utilisation factor of 0·48 and a maintenance factor of 0·8, determine the general level of illumination provided by the luminaires.

9. A machine shop 50m by 27m is illuminated to a level of 300 lx by incandescent luminaires which have an efficacy 16 lm/W. It is decided to replace these luminaires by fluorescent luminaires having an efficacy of 40 lm/W so that the overall level of illumination remains the same. Estimate the saving in the cost of electrical energy per 8-hour shift assuming:
    (a) that all the luminaires are in use during the 8 hours;
    (b) utilisation and maintenance factors are the same for both types of luminaires at 0·5 and 0·8 respectively;
    (c) electrical energy costs 7p per unit.

10. A warehouse is 30m by 20m. Illumination is to be provided by a number of 1000W luminaires having an efficacy of 16 lm/W and a spacing-height ratio of 1·5. The luminaires are suspended 4m above the working surface. The utilisation factor is 0·53 and the maintenance factor is 0·75.
    (a) Estimate the number of luminaires required;
    (b) Determine the general level of illumination produced.

11. (i) Explain the points that should be considered when planning the electric lighting of one of the following:

    (a) a workshop with rows of benches for small assembly work;

    (b) a large drawing office.

(ii) An office 20m by 50m needs an average illumination at desk level of 400 lx. The following alternatives are available:

    (a) 80W fluorescent luminaires emitting 2800 lumens when new;

    (b) 150W tungsten filament luminaires emitting 13 lm/W when new.

Calculate the number of luminaires needed for each alternative assuming the utilisation factor for the room to be 0·6 and the maintenance factor to be 0·85.   (C & G)

12. A workshop measuring 15m by 25m by 3·5m high, used for simple bench fitting of small parts, needs a general illumination at bench level of 400 lx. The following schemes are suggested:

    (a) 80W fluorescent luminaires emitting 40 lm/W;

    (b) 200W tungsten filament luminaires emitting 13 lm/W.

Assuming the utilisation factor to be 0·65 and the maintenance factor to be 0·8, calculate the number of luminaires to be installed for each scheme.

For each case draw a diagram giving your suggested layout of the luminaires showing their spacing and mounting height.

  (C & G)

UTILISATION OF ELECTRIC POWER IV
PLANNING OF HEATING SCHEMES

References: **Power and energy.**

              Specific heat capacity.

              Heat loss.

Examples

A. A storage heater contains 0·1 m³ of water. The 240-V heating element produces a temperature rise of 85 degC in 1½ hours and the efficiency of the device is 82%. Calculate the rating of the heater in watts and the resistance of its element. The specific heat of water is 4187 joules per kilogram per degree Celsius.

In a heating operation

Energy in the form of heat = mass × temperature rise
× specific heat

$$Q = m \times (\theta_2 - \theta_1) \times c$$

where m is the mass of substance in kg

c is its specific heat in J/(kgdegC)

θ_2 and θ_1 are the upper and lower temperatures in °C

1 m³ of water weights 10^3 kg

substituting the given values

$$Q = 0.1 \times 10^3 \, \text{kg} \times 85 \, \text{degC} \times 4187 \frac{\text{J}}{\text{kgdegC}}$$

$$= 0.1 \times 10^3 \times 85 \times 4187 \, \text{J}$$

and the energy to be supplied

$$W = 0.1 \times 10^3 \times 85 \times 4187 \times \frac{100}{82}$$

(allowing for inefficiency)

$$= 43\,402\,000 \, \text{J}$$

This energy is supplied over a period of 1½ hours, that is,

$$1\tfrac{1}{2} \times 3600 \text{ seconds}$$

energy supplied per second

$$= \frac{43\,402\,000 \, \text{J}}{1.5 \times 3600 \, \text{s}}$$

$$= 8037 \text{W}$$

or 8.037 kW

which is the power rating of the
element.

The relationship between power and resistance is

$$P = \frac{U^2}{R}$$

$$8037 = \frac{240^2}{R}$$

$$R = \frac{240^2}{8037}$$

$$= 7 \cdot 17\Omega$$

which is the resistance of the element.

B. A room has dimensions 4m by 6mn by 2·5m. Electric heaters are to be provided to produce an average temperature rise of 8 degC. Calculate the rating of the heaters required assuming two changes of air occur per hour and that 40% of their output is wasted.

The density of air is 1·28 kg/m³ and its specific heat is 1000 J/(kg degC).

Volume of room $= 4 \times 6 \times 2 \cdot 5$

$$= 60\text{m}^3$$

mass of air in the room

$$= 60\,\cancel{\text{m}} \times 1 \cdot 28\,\frac{\text{kg}}{\cancel{\text{m}}}$$

$$= 76 \cdot 8\text{ kg}$$

Heat content of the air for each hour

$$Q = 2 \times 76 \cdot 8\,\cancel{\text{kg}} \times 8\,\cancel{\text{degC}} \times 1000\,\frac{\text{J}}{\cancel{\text{kg degC}}}$$

$$= 2 \times 76 \cdot 8 \times 8 \times 1000\text{ J}$$

153

Electrical energy required per hour

$$W = 2 \times 76{\cdot}8 \times 8 \times 1000 \times \frac{100}{60}$$

(only 60% of the energy is usefully employed)

$$= 20{\cdot}5 \times 10^5 \text{ joules per hour}$$

$$= \frac{20{\cdot}5 \times 10^5}{3600} \text{ J/s}$$

$$= \underline{570\text{W}}$$

C. A building is 6·5m by 8m and has ceiling height 3m. The windows have total area 7 m² and there are wooden doors of total area 3·5 m². Allowing two complete changes of air per hour, calculate the power required to maintain a 20 degC temperature difference between the inside and outside of the building. Heat transmission coefficients in watts per square metre per degree Celsius are:

Brick (walls)   1·88

Concrete (floor)   1·13

Plaster (ceiling)   2·84

Wood   3·98

Glass   5·4

The density of air is 1·28 kg/m³ and its specific heat is 1000 J/(kgdegC).

The calculation is performed in two sections:

(i) To calculate the heat losses through walls, etc.

Area of brick wall = total area − area of doors

− area of windows

$$= (2 \times 6{\cdot}5 \times 3) + (2 \times 8 \times 3)$$

$$- 3{\cdot}5 - 7$$

$$= 76{\cdot}5 \text{ m}^2$$

Let P_b be the power wasted in the form of heat through the brick

$$P_b = 1 \cdot 88 \frac{W}{m^2 \, \text{degC}} \times 76 \cdot 5 \, m^2 \times 20 \, \text{degC}$$

$$= 1 \cdot 88 \times 76 \cdot 5 \times 20$$

$$= 2877 W$$

Similarly for the wood

$$P_W = 3 \cdot 98 \times 3 \cdot 5 \times 20$$

$$= 278 \cdot 6 W$$

and for the glass

$$P_G = 5 \cdot 4 \times 7 \times 20$$

$$= 756 W$$

and for the concrete

$$P_C = 1 \cdot 13 \times 8 \times 6 \cdot 5 \times 20$$

$$= 1175 W$$

and for the plaster

$$P_P = 2 \cdot 84 \times 8 \times 6 \cdot 5 \times 20$$

$$= 2954 W$$

Total power loss

$$= 2877 + 278 \cdot 6 + 756 + 1175$$
$$+ 2954$$

$$= 8041 W$$

(ii) To calculate the heat required to warm the air; mass of air within the room

$$= \text{volume} \times \text{density}$$

$$= 6 \cdot 5 \times 8 \times 3 \, m^3 \times 1 \cdot 28 \, \frac{kg}{m^3}$$

$$= 199 \cdot 68 \, kg$$

Heat required to raise the temperature of twice this
mass of air through 20 degC

$$= \text{mass} \times \text{temperature rise} \times \text{specific heat}$$

$$= 199 \cdot 68 \; \cancel{\text{kg}} \times 20 \; \cancel{\text{degC}} \times 1000 \; \frac{\text{J}}{\cancel{\text{kg degC}}} \times 2$$

$$= 7\,987\,200 \text{ joules per hour}$$

$$= \frac{7\,987\,200}{3600} \text{ joules per second}$$

$$= 2219\text{W}$$

Total power required

$$= 2219 + 8041$$

$$= 10\,260\text{W}$$

$$\text{or} \quad \underline{10 \cdot 26 \text{ kW}}$$

Exercises 17

Specific heat of water 4187 J/(kg degC)
Specific heat of air   1000 J/(kg degC)
Density of air   1·28 kg/m³

1. With the aid of sketches, describe the operation of a thermostat-
   ically controlled immersion heater as fitted into domestic hot
   water systems.
   A 240-V storage heater contains 0·055 m³ of water. The
   temperature of the water is raised from 18°C to 88°C in 1¼
   hours with an efficiency of 88%. Assuming the current remains
   constant throughout the run, find the resistance of the element
   during the operation, the number of units used and the nominal
   size of the heater in kW.

2. Describe with clear sketches, a free-outlet electric water heater
   as installed over a wash basin or kitchen sink, and explain how
   it works.
   A heater of this type rated at 750W, holds 0·007 m³ of water.
   If it takes 58 minutes to raise the temperature of the water from
   20°C to 90°C, calculate the efficiency of the water heater.

3. A domestic hot-water cylinder holds 0.136 m^3 of water and is fitted with a 3-kW heater. Assuming an efficiency of 70%, calculate the time required to raise the temperature of the water from 5°C to 70°C.

4. An industrial process requires 0.2 m^3 per hour of liquid of specific heat 2000 J/(kg degC) and density 900 kg/m^3 to be raised in temperature by 80 degC. Assuming that 35% of the heat supplied is wasted, calculate the rating of the heater in kW required for the process. Determine also the resistance of the element for operation from a 240-V supply.

5. Write a short account of the design factors to be taken into account when considering the electrical heating of a room.

   A room 11m by 6m by 3.5m high, is heated by means of low-temperature tubular heaters with a total loading of 9 kW. Assume that 40% of the heat supplied is used to heat the air in the room.

   Calculate the average temperature rise of the air if there are two complete changes of air per hour.

6. Describe with sketches, the construction and operation of a domestic-type thermal storage room heater.

   A room 5m by 3.5m by 3m high is heated by a thermal storage heater. The heater takes in electrical energy during the night from 2200 hrs to 0700 hrs and releases the stored heat during the day from 0700 hrs to 2200 hrs. The average temperature rise in the room is 20 degC and there are two complete changes of air in each hour. Assuming that 45% of the energy supplied to the heater is used to heat the air in the room, calculate (a) the kWh input to the heater in 24 hours, (b) the kW rating of the heater.

7. A room is 5m by 4m and is 3m high. It is required to maintain the temperature within the room at 9 degC above that of the surroundings and there are to be two complete changes of air per hour. Calculate the rating of the heaters required assuming that the system is 65% efficient.

8. A workshop 13m by 6.5m with ceiling height 3.5m has a window area of 35 m^2 and a door area of 10 m^2. The workshop is to be heated electrically so that the average temperature inside is maintained at 18°C when the temperature outside is 0°C.

   Using the information given in example C, calculate the power required in kW on the assumption that there will be two complete changes of air per hour.

9. A glass house on a concrete base is 6.5m long. The end section is that of a rectangle 2.5m wide and 1.5m high surmounted by a

triangle 0·75m high. Using the information given in example C and assuming 1½ complete changes of air per hour, calculate the rating of the heaters necessary to maintain the inside of the building at a temperature 17 degC above that of the outside.

10. A brick building with concrete floor and plaster ceiling is 25m long, 10m wide and 3·5m high. There are windows of total area 36 m² and wooden doors of total area 16 m². It is required to maintain the temperature inside the building 18 degC above that of the outside with two changes of air per hour by using electric heaters. Use the information given in example C to determine the rating of the heaters required.

ANSWERS

Exercises 1—*page* 14

1. (a) $10 = 12I_1 - 6I_2$
        $0 = -6I_1 + 15I_2$
   (b) $0 = 16I_1 - 6I_2$
        $-10 = -6I_1 + 11I_2$
   (c) $6 = 13I_1 - 4I_2$
        $-8 = -4I_1 + 16I_2$
   (d) $-2 = 17I_1 - 2I_2$
        $4 = -2I_1 + 17I_2$
   (e) $0 = 10I_1 - 5I_2 - 4I_3$
        $0 = -5I_1 + 10I_2 - 3I_3$
        $2 = -4I_1 - 3I_2 + 8I_3$
   (f) $2 = 7I_1 - 4I_2$
        $0 = -4I_1 + 22I_2 - 6I_3$
        $-2 = -6I_2 + 18I_3$

2. (a) $I_{BA} = I_{AF} = I_{FE} = \frac{1}{7}$A; $I_{BC} = I_{CD} = I_{BE} = \frac{3}{21}$A;
        $I_{EB} = \frac{5}{21}$A
   (b) $I_{BA} = I_{AF} = I_{FE} = 0.4$A; $I_{DE} = I_{CD} = I_{BC} = 0.2$A;
        $I_{EB} = 0.6$A
   (c) $I_{BA} = I_{AH} = I_{HG} = 3.428$A; $I_{CB} = I_{GF} = 1.875$A;
        $I_{DC} = I_{FE} = I_{ED} = 5.938$A; $I_{GB} = 1.563$A; $I_{CF} = 4.063$A

3. $I_{BD} = \frac{1}{14}$A

4. $I_{10} = 0.563$A; 5·63V

5. Current through battery of internal resistance $1\Omega = 0.25$A
   Current through battery of internal resistance $2\Omega = 0.125$A
   Total charging current = 0·375A

6.

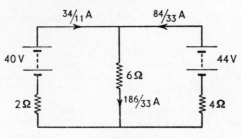

7. 3mA, D to B
8. (a) 49Ω; 6·428A. (b) 25Ω
9. I_{AB} = 240A; I_{BC} = 180A; I_{CD} = 100A; U_B = 225V;
   U_C = 214V; U_D = 210V
10. I_{AB} = 158·3A; I_{BC} = 98·3A; I_{CD} = 18·3A; I_{DA} = 81·7A;
    U_B = 227V; U_C = 221V; U_D = 220V
11. I_{PQ} = 77·5A; I_{QR} = 7·5A; I_{RP} = −42·5A;
    U_O = 231V; U_R = 230V
12.

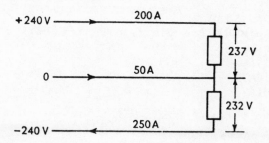

Exercises 2—*page* 26

1. (a) 18·7Ω; (b) 12·82A; (c) 0·802 (lead); (d) U_R = 193V,
   U_L = 128V, U_C = 272V
2. 1·523A
5. (a) 6·2A; (b) U_R = 149V; U_L = 312V; U_C = 123V; (c) 31·4Hz;
   10A
6. (a) 19·45A; 3030W; 0·648 lag; (b) 169 μF
7. 24 μF, 0·625 lead; 425 μF, 0·625 lag.
8. (i) 0·318H; (ii) 48·9 μF; (iii) 99V
9. 100 Hz, 34·7 Hz
10. (i) 26·5 Hz; (ii) 25A; (iii) $U_L = U_C$ = 2080V; U_R = 100V

Exercises 3—*page* 39

1. 1·41A (lag).
2. 2·78A; 0·86 (lag).
3. 3·49A; 0·92 (lag).
4. 0·609A; 0·992 (lead).
5. R = 163Ω; L = 0·068 H
6. I_C = 15A; I_L = 13·6A; I = 17·4A; 0·99 (lag).
7. 10·6 μF

8. 87·4 Hz

9. 1·71A

10. 55·2 μF

Exercises 4—*page* 45

1. 4·62A; 2561W
2. 1·697A; 864W
3. $I_R = 9.6A$; $I_Y = 18.5A$; $I_B = 12A$; 5448W
4. 10A; 5760W
5. 7·21A; 5280W
6. $I_R = 104.1A$; $I_Y = 125A$; $I_B = 50A$; $I_N = 67.1A$
7. 55·18A
8. 1·757A
9. 6·56A
10. 7·51A

Exercises 5—*page* 49

1. (a) 8A; 8A; 5760W
   (b) 13·83A; 24A; 17 280W
2. 19·21A; 7388W
3. (a) 5·37A; 3894W
   (b) 3·106A; 1302W
4. (a) 2·25A; 0·469 (lag); 759·4W
   (b) 6·75A; 0·469 (lag); 2278W
5. (a) 7·2Ω; (b) 21·6Ω
6. (a) 884 μF; (b) 295 μF
7. $I_{RY} = 6.92A$; $I_{YB} = 8.3A$; $I_{BR} = 13.04A$; 5625W
8. (a) 17·2A; (b) 29·8A; (c) 20 900W.

Exercises 6—*page* 55

1. 22 kW; 5 kVAr (lag); 22·6 kVA; 0·974 (lag).
2. 0·885 (lag); 95·7A
3. (a) 34·9A; (b) 28·2A; 0·87 (lag).
4. 30·1 kW; 21·3 kVAr; 36·9 kVA; 0·82 (lag); 51·3A
5. (a) 6·68 kVAr (lead); (b) (i) 123 μF; (ii) 41·2 μF
6. (a) 89 kVA; (b) 0·807 (lag); (c) 71·7 kW; (d) 370A
7. 191A; 0·956 (lag).
8. 147 μF; 441 μF
9. 148 μF

10.

	kVA	kW	kVAr	p.f.	Line current
a	15	12	9 (lag)	0·8 (lag)	20·9A
b	12	12	0	1·0	16·7A
c	8	0	8 (lead)	0	11·1A
d	14·4	11·5	8·63 (lag)	0·8 (lag)	20A
overall values	36·8	35·5	9·63 (lag)	0·965 (lag)	51·2A

11. (i) 49 kW; (ii) 0·97.

(Hint: $W_1 + W_2 = \sqrt{3}\ U_L I_L \cos \phi$

$W_1 - W_2 = U_L I_L \sin \phi$

$\sin \phi / \cos \phi = \tan \phi = \sqrt{3}(W_1 - W_2)/\ W_1 + W_2$

hence ϕ and $\cos \phi$)

(iii) 50·5 kVA; (iv) 70·3A

12. 7·72p

13. 29·6 kW

14. £35715; 5·95; £37338; 6·22p

Exercises 7—*page 69*

1. 401 V; 3·51%; 756 W

2. (a) 425 V; (b) 1110W

3. 11·7 V

4. 95 mm²

5. 451 mm²; 500mm²; 4·51 V.

6. 5·8 V

7. 70 mm²

8. 25 mm²

9. 70 mm²

10. 25A

11. (a) 16·7 A; (b) 20 A;
(c) 19·97mV/A/m;
(d) 29·34 A; (e) 6mm²;
(f) 3·2 V; (g) 25mm.

12. (a) (i) 1213 A; (ii) 0·25 s;
(iii) 0·41 Ω: (iv) 585 A; (v) 3s; (b)
0·44 Ω.

Exercises 8—*page 81*

2. 0·000 442 Wb

3. 0·8 T

4. 0·8 T

5. 420 At/m

6. 700 At

7. 500

8. 0·551 A

9. (*a*) 0·0251 T; (*b*) 0·132 T; (*c*) 0·943 T

12. 227 000 At/m

13. 4·86 A

14. about 1A

15. about 4A

16. about 0·35 mWb

17. 0·397A

18. 0·767A

19. 4·61 mWb

20. 0·462 mWb   **21.** 905 At
22. 0·8 A   **23.** 0·645 A

Exercises 9—*page* 89

3. 10 H

5. 0.03J; 0·005 J; 500 J;
0·0002 J

7. 150 Ω

4. 1.42 ms

6. 240 J

8. (a) 108 H; (b) 1667 J;
(c) 90 Ω (d) 833·5 J

Exercises 10—*page* 94

1. (a) 82·5 A; (b) 259 V;
(c) 1961 W

3. 0·036 Wb

5. 12·35 rev/s

7. (i) 6·94 kW; (ii) 69·8 Nm

9. (i) 73·46%; (ii) 1084 W

11. (i) 105·67 A; (ii) 254·12 V
(iii) field 360 W; armature
1340 W.

2. 213 V

4. 12·63 rev/s

6. 255 V

8. (i) 2 A; (ii) 30 A; (iii) 243 V

10. 234 V; 238·4 V

12. 25 A

13. (i) 75 A; (ii) 244·13 V;
(iii) 3·09 A; (iv) 78·09 A;
(v) 249·13 V

Exercises 11—*page* 106

1. 190 Nm

3. 19·88 rev/s

5. 17 A

7. 45·71 rev/s

9. 16·78 A; 215 V; 63·13%;
31·9 Nm

11. 23·7 rev/s

13. 4147 W; 71·5%

15. 4·88 Ω

17. 1·96 Ω

2. 23·83 rev/s

4. 1410 Nm

6. 13·33 rev/s

8. 7·78 kW; 74%; 113 Nm

10. 9·87 rev/s

12. 86·4%

14. 82·1%

16. 1·71 Ω

18. 6·3 Ω

Exercises 12—*page* 112

1. 1648W

3. 57·67 Nm

5. 89·2A

7. 78%; 0·692 (lag).

9. 5·269 kW; 16·4A

2. 73·9 Nm

4. 110·3 Nm

6. 2·18A

8. 12·7 rev/min; 2575 Nm

10. 24·7A; 130 Nm

Exercises 13—*page* 124

1. 32·7.

2. 12·1A

3. 375V; 162·5V
4. 0·541 T
5. 1200.
6. 4800.
7. 5·39A; 0·372 (lag).
8. $I_W = 0.8A$; $I_\mu = 3.92A$
9. $I_\mu = 1.97A$; $I_W = 0.36A$
10. (i) 3·68A; (ii) 4·42A; (iii) 2·54A
12. (i) 95·4%; (ii) 94·9%.
13. (i) 93·9%; (ii) 92·8%.
14. (i) 99%; (ii) 98·9%.
15. 30·35 degC
16. 21·9 kW; 95·6%.
17. 98·04%.
18. 83·9%.
19. 96·7%.
20. 3·614%.
21. 228V
22. (A) 15·38 MVA; 269 A
23. 9 MVA; 418
　　　(C) 23·9 MVA; 418A

Exercises 14—*page* 139

1. (*a*) 53·1 pF; (*b*) 3983 pC; 0·149 μJ; (*c*) 0·332 μC/m²; 50 kV/m
2. 83·78 mm
3. 0·01C; 0·5 μJ; (*a*) 0·25 μJ; (*b*) 1 μJ
4. (*a*) 1·88 μF; (*b*) 450 μC; (*c*) 150V; 90V; (*d*) 0·034 J; 0·02 J
5. 8 μF; 2·4 μF
6. 60 μF
7. (i) 3·7 μF; 111V; 74V; 56V; (ii) 36 μF; 240V
8. 12 μF
9. $Q_{64} = 6400\ \mu$C　　$W_{64} = 0.32$ J
　　$Q_{12} = 2400\ \mu$C　　$W_{12} = 0.24$ J
　　$Q_{20} = 4000\ \mu$C　　$W_{20} = 0.4$ J
10. (*a*) 12 000 μC; 1·2 J; (*b*) 120V; 0·72 J.
11. 255 pF
12. 81·52 pF
15. 8·6 μF

Exercises 15—*page* 145

1. 15·6 lx; 8 lx
2. 4·77 lx
3. 27 lx
4. (*a*) 28·8 lx; (*b*) 28·7 lx; (*c*) 28 lx
5 (*a*) 111 lx; (*b*) 50·4 lx; (*c*) 47·2 lx
6 100 lx; 71·6 lx; 35·4 lx; 17·1 lx
7. 47·2 lx; 51·2 lx
8. 1340 cd

Exercises 16—*page* 149

1. (*a*) 5·26 kW; (*b*) 1·84 kW
2. (*a*) 2·857 kW; (*b*) £13·23.
3. 36.
4. 15 kW
5. 24.
8. 123 lx
9. £21·27.
10. (*a*) 15; (*b*) 159 lx
11. (*a*) 280; (*b*) 402.
12. (*a*) 90; (*b*) 110.

Exercises 17—*page* 156

1. 14·1Ω; 5·1; 4 kW
2. (*a*) 2·857 kW; (*b*) £13·23
3. 4 hours 53 minutes;
4. 12·3 kW; 4·68Ω
5. 22 degC
6. (*a*) 24·9 kWh; (b) 2·77 kW
7. 591W
8. 17·2 kW
9. £21·27.
10. 28·6 kW

164